The most r

is p

RISE.
AMAZING WOMAN.
RISE.

The Eight Essential Powers of the Feminine Heart

MARSH ENGLE

Featuring the transformational insights and inspiration of influential
mentors, entrepreneurs and change makers.

LEADERS IN GLOBAL PUBLISHING

Published by Motivational Press, Inc.
1777 Aurora Road
Melbourne, Florida, 32935
www.MotivationalPress.com

Manufactured in the United States of America.

ISBN: 978-1-62865-609-1

CONTENTS

THE PREFACE 9

THE INTRODUCTION 16

BEFORE YOU GET STARTED. 35

Chapter One. 40

   THE ESSENTIAL POWER TO EVOLVE

Chapter Two. 55

   THE ESSENTIAL POWER OF SELF-LOVE

Chapter Three. 67

   THE ESSENTIAL POWER OF INTUITION

Chapter Four. 82

   THE ESSENTIAL POWER OF PRESENCE

Chapter Five. 95

   THE ESSENTIAL POWER OF BALANCE

Chapter Six. 110

   THE ESSENTIAL POWER OF SELF-AUTHORITY

Chapter Seven 126

   THE ESSENTIAL POWER OF CONNECTION

Chapter Eight 143

   THE ESSENTIAL POWER OF RADIANT ACHIEVEMENT

Chapter Nine. 165

   I AM RISING

I AM RISING 168

Intentional Statements

WRITE YOUR OWN. 182

I AM RISING

ACKNOWLEDGMENTS. 187

ABOUT MARSH ENGLE 189

Elegant and creative. Courageous and confident.
Boldly inspired. Genuine and intelligent.
At the core of your feminine heart is the inextinguishable
spirit of the amazing woman you are and have ALWAYS been.

Dedication

This book is dedicated to you,
a woman embracing her feminine heart
so the world might be blessed by the presence
of an amazing woman in all of her elegant power to lead.

The methods described within this book are the contributor's personal thoughts, experiences and opinions. The intention of the book is to broaden the reader's perspective. The content is not intended to be a definitive set of instructions. The author makes no representations or warranties of any kind with respect to this book or its contents, including advice for a particular purpose. Always use your own intuition and common sense. You may discover there are other methods and materials to accomplish the same end results. It is recommended before you begin any change in your lifestyle in any way, to consult a licensed professional ensuring you are doing what is best for your situation or circumstance. This book provides content related to education, creativity, meditation, mindset, success and leadership topics. As such, use of this book implies your acceptance of this disclaimer.

"There is a new wave of women's leadership emerging. And, it is being led by the woman who knows her greatest power to create goes well beyond the day-to-day striving for results — she knows her true power to contribute to the world in significant ways is one that expresses her heart, enlivens her creativity and stretches her spirit."

THE PREFACE

T HE FEMININE HEART is the source of true power, intelligence, insight and understanding. Tap into this power and you will access the ability to transform your views of money, success, happiness, and fulfillment – you unlock hidden talents, uncover new meaning and amplify the significance of your purpose. In essence, accessing the power of the feminine heart moves you beyond old, outdated concepts about your capacities to create and lead, becoming less about rules and expectations and more about expressing your authentic voice, at home and at work.

These 8 Essential Powers Of The Feminine Heart Are The Future Of Success In Leadership

More than a book, RISE, AMAZING WOMAN, RISE is a call for women everywhere to rise and claim the essential powers of the feminine heart, as the super-powers of leadership they truly are.

This book joins together a collection of transformational authors, in a shared intention to accelerate an ever-evolving dialogue about the culture of women's success in leadership. Throughout the pages, you will link arms with eight influential mentors, entrepreneurs and change makers who guide you step-by-step into the essential powers of the feminine heart. Together we will challenge old, outdated perceptions. We will redefine the feminine heart as a source of power that should be embraced, rather than hidden, denied or considered a weakness.

For years, even the most successful women in business succeeded by leaning heavily on their masculine side feeling it necessary to bring their hard-charging, over-thinking face to the fore. Today, though, more and more women — and many men, too — are embracing the positive change and transformation that can only take place by putting their feminine qualities first.

A great and profound shift takes place once you learn the essential powers of the feminine heart.

You will stop allowing anyone or anything to diminish, limit, or discourage you from being ALL you are.

You will recognize your self-worth is yours to define – that your destiny is yours to create.

You will break free from attitudes, people, and situations that dilute your creative spirit.

You will rise, amazing woman. You will rise!

However, to make this shift we must understand we're not here for the small things. We are here to cultivate every ability. Access every creative capacity. Stand strong in our values. Get vocal about all we stand for.

For this very reason, for the writing of RISE AMAZING WOMAN RISE, I've brought together a collaborative of forward-moving influential change makers – each bringing a depth of insight within each chapter, offering an exploration of our feminine heart in the context of success in leadership. Through their writing, we will see how the qualities of the feminine heart manifest through eight essential powers. These unforgettable lessons from inspired mentors will motivate you to liberate your own hidden capacities, deepen the clarity of your inner voice, and fulfill your highest destiny.

THE ESSENTIAL POWERS OF THE FEMININE HEART

THE ESSENTIAL POWER TO EVOLVE

"When we evolve together, we rise above the predefined cultural conditioning that would have us playing small and silent. We rise above the negative chatter by focusing our intentions on bringing more love and light into the world.

And today, the world needs to hear our voices that can soften perspectives and lift us all up with love and compassion."

Theresa Wray

THE ESSENTIAL POWER OF SELF-LOVE

"There are times in our lives where a revolution of the soul brings the revelations needed to guide us back to self-love. A revolution of the soul can look like a crisis: the end of a marriage, the death of a child or partner, or even life-threatening illnesses.

Our soul is calling us to awaken. And so, it begins one revelation at a time.

Beginning with one act of self-love at a time, line upon line, at every age, though the beauty of self-love we begin to rise."

Pamela Nebeker

THE ESSENTIAL POWER OF INTUITION

"When we honor our intuition, we free up our energy because we are no longer, or are less often, defaulting to trying to control our circumstances or figure things out. Instead, we trust ourselves and the moment at hand and get curious about what is being offered through it."

Wendy L. Yost

THE ESSENTIAL POWER OF PRESENCE

"Presence comes into our world when we are ready to stand still and be in our power. The power comes from being excited to live in this moment and to allow yourself to be within the moment and listen."

Conni Ponturo

THE ESSENTIAL POWER OF BALANCE

"As we embrace lifestyles of balance, we open our hearts and minds to living lives of service. As we recognize that all life is connected, we make more conscious choices, taking into account how they will impact the earth and other communities.

When we open our hearts to empathy and are able to be present to the impact of our choices on others, we become part of the solution for our highest evolution."

Heather Salmon

THE ESSENTIAL POWER OF SELF-AUTHORITY

"When we are not in our self-authority we lean towards recklessness.

We abandon our sense of worth. Underestimate our value, and feel disconnected from all that we are.

But, when anchored in the power of self-authority, we consider, discern, and make choices that are in alignment centered and in harmony with our heart and our mind and our spirit."

Patrina Wisdom

THE ESSENTIAL POWER OF CONNECTION

"Collectively we as women are experiencing an epidemic of disconnection right now. Disconnection to ourselves, our physiology, our hearts, our deepest drives, and needs."

Dena Breslin

THE ESSENTIAL POWER OF RADIANT ACHIEVEMENT

"Radiant Achievement is about doing your absolute best to bring forth the seeds of your potential, to bring forth the next level of your own evolution and all your soul is asking of you. To be and become the fullness of the woman you were born to be."

Christine Howard

Rise Amazing Woman Rise
brings into balance the single greatest superpower
for creating success in leadership:
The Power of the Feminine Heart.

Above all, through the words and teachings you will experience on the pages of RISE AMAZING WOMAN RISE, you will be immersed in a new and empowered relationship with your own feminine heart – an ever-evolving strength that exhibits presence, self-love, balance, self-authority, intuitive intelligence, and radiant achievement.

In essence, RISE AMAZING WOMAN RISE signifies the emergence of our single greatest superpower for creating success in leadership: *The power of the feminine heart.*

It's what the world needs more than ever.

Marsh Engle

THE INTRODUCTION

JANUARY 15, 2019, marks the 20-year anniversary of the day I first began to define the vision and the message that would become the foundation and premise for my life's work. Little did I know the myriad of changes destined to take place in the years to follow. Or, that the heart and spirit of the AMAZING WOMAN message of *feminine success* and *feminine leadership* would be amplified into a global movement accelerating the transformation of thousands of women.

> "The essential powers of the feminine heart can and will transform the world!"

Even today, especially today, much is changing in the lives of women. From how we see things, to how we do things, we are at the center of creating a significant shift in our culture, our lives, our communities, and the world.

We are claiming our essential Self power, bringing to the fore elevated actions, deepened connections, and higher contribution – embodying both the internal and external aspects of the invisible power and creative capacities of the feminine heart.

However this approach to leadership and success was not always easily accepted. And was often met with great resistance. Introducing the qualities of the feminine heart into an environment steeped in masculine ways required a new definition of leadership and success. It required a significant change in our ways of thinking.

In 1999, early in the development of a new concept in women's conferences called *Amazing Woman's Day,* several advisers told me directly, "Your program looks and sounds innovative and significant, but no one in business or otherwise is going to take your work seriously if you use the language *Feminine Success* or *Feminine Leadership* in the description of your conference."

To me the use of the word *feminine* placed next to the word *success* – or, blending of the word *feminine* with the word *leadership* – felt natural and relevant – and, even more, it felt necessary. But, after further exploration and in the context of success in leadership, I found it was the word *feminine* that had a tendency to strike many as being soft, emotional and weak.

Of course, I decided to move forward with the conference, including the use of *feminine success* and *feminine leadership* to describe it. In fact, the principles of *feminine success* became the primary distinctions of the Amazing Woman's Day Conference series, bringing forth *feminine leadership* and placing it front and center throughout the conference. And I did it full knowing I'd face some resistance. And, that was most definitely the case. But I stayed true to the vision. The success of the conference carried on for ten consecutive years, visiting 3 countries and over 50 U.S. cities, impacting thousands upon thousands of women's lives. Ever since I've made it my intention to be loyal to the mission of introducing the essential qualities of the feminine heart into career development and business leadership – always looking to find as much compelling evidence as possible to prove the essential bridge between creativity, feminine esteem, and practices that bring a greater equilibrium and influence of both the mind *and* the heart.

The answer is to bring into balance an impeccable acceptance of the feminine heart and integrate its' essential power into the culture of our success in leadership.

OWNING THE POWER OF THE FEMININE HEART AT WORK.

In all honesty, as I look back, I'm reminded there was a time that I too, questioned the power of my feminine nature, often conforming to the judgment that it was too soft, too emotional, and too weak. My early days as a budding media executive, took place when the outlook for women in America was just beginning to change. I was one of the few women at the *big table*, a business environment primarily populated by men, who were more heavily focused on the bottom line, than creativity and teamwork (it was more like *my way or the highway.* Or, *every 'man' for himself*). Anything resembling intuition or inspiration or passion, found very little place in business.

So, what did I do? I conformed.

In those days' women role models or mentors in media were few. And, those who were available tended to readily conform to the rules of the time. I went along with the crowd. I dressed the part with a closet filled with pinstriped business suits, shoulder pads, and scarfs that I often tied at the neck. I pulled my hair back. To be taken seriously as a business woman, I found it necessary to filter my naturally enthusiastic personality into a stern appearance and behavior.

> "Trying to be a man is a waste of a woman."
> *Allison Pearson*

Stepping away from media, to open my own marketing agency became my first step in realizing there's another way of doing it…of building a business, of creating success, and of leadership. From the moment the doors of my new business swung open, it became less about the expected ways of achieving and more about innovating in ways that had never been done before. Here I found there was plenty of space to bring my feminine strengths to the table and be more of my true self. In fact, I found that my feminine strengths became my biggest and most valued distinction – trademarks of my success and of my leadership – creativity, innovation, collaboration, intuitive decision-making, and so much more. I excelled and so did my business.

I can now easily see the creation of *Amazing Woman's Day* was my way to give back what I wished I had when I was struggling to rise in my own expression of *feminine success* and *feminine leadership*: designing an environment for women to be themselves. I wasn't only looking for a means to break through a ceiling...I was looking for ways to create a cultural shift in the value of our feminine nature...to create a movement where women link arms to rise in feminine esteem...to bring our power into balance.

And, to this day, this remains to be the focus of my work. It is what I speak and teach. It's my passion to bring it to broadcast and carry it onto stages. I write about it. And coach women to design careers, business, and brands based on it.

Today, we need not look far to recognize the heightening value of those qualities most widely regarded as feminine – skills such as empathy, intuition, flexibility and collaboration – have gone unrecognized for too long.

It's time for a radiant revolution, a radiant evolution of our
definition of success in leadership.

A genuine rumbling has begun; its theme is the recognition of our innate capacities to create real and lasting change. Outdated attitudes are dropping away. Competitiveness and unfairness are being challenged. And, like any revolution, the results can give way to an enlightened new direction, a cultural shift, and an expansion in consciousness.

A shift is underway, a fueling of a vast movement of women,
who no longer accept the imbalance that exists in success in
leadership.

There is a marked necessity for an evolved approach, one
that allows for a partnership with creativity, innovation, and
purpose – essential powers of the feminine heart.

When we look around, it can quickly be recognized that the cultural shift that is taking place goes well beyond an individual issue. In fact, it's the call for this cultural shift that is bringing us to our feet and moving us into action. It's the innate wisdom of this shift that's catalyzing a motivation of women to step up and share their once suppressed voices and truths. It is the marked necessity for an elevated approach, that's defining a new paradigm of success in leadership – one that allows for a partnership with balance, presence, inner-authority and radiant achievement – each serving as an essential power of the feminine heart.

However, to fully make the shift, we must each do our own part. We must set free our uncensored truth. And give rise to an unapologetic self-expression that serves as the catalyst for genuine, lasting change. Rising from a position of perceived weakness, to one of strength – transforming ancient feminine wounds into a source of higher self-empowerment — these are important transformational shifts in everyone's life – and especially now.

The fact is, embracing the qualities of the feminine heart has been a running thread in human culture for thousands upon thousands of years. But each generation must reinterpret it, redefine it, and find ways to embody it. In a time where daily demands and distractions tend to be the rule, embodying the essential powers of the feminine heart requires going deeper into our self-awareness – pausing to take the time to create the change – and assigning a high value to the change that is being created.

"At the heart and soul of our most fierce feminine power is a mighty desire to make a difference. It's the call to transform.

It's the call to lead. It's a call to act upon creating the transformation we know we can create.

Most of all, it's the call to leave a lasting legacy of love in the world."

Within the pages of RISE, AMAZING WOMAN, RISE you will find an unshakable bridge to make the shift – to reveal your true self – to rise up and stand strong in the vibrancy of your highest potentials – to touch the core of your sacred purpose – and, to establish a partnership with the grace of your feminine heart. *The result:* A fostering of the tremendous values and strengths within you – access to a touchstone of your innovative creative nature – a healing of outdated feminine wounds – and expressive freedom.

To be receptive to the powers of the feminine heart – to gain access to the touchstone of our vast creative nature – a healing of outdated feminine wounds must take place.

I know those periods of feeling painfully disconnected, as though something is missing – experiencing feelings of insignificance, fear, anger, isolation and loneliness, and most of all, shame.

On the individual level, the disconnection from the feminine heart can be devastating – the impact runs deep. In many ways we've been bred to doubt ourselves, continually questioning our innate callings to create. By the time we begin to sincerely consider bringing out our gifts and talents and sharing them with others, so many are plagued by uncertainties and hesitations that silently steal and diminish our power on all levels.

I doubt there is anyone of us who cannot benefit from healing wounds to our feminine heart and deepening a connection with the most sacred, forgotten, denied part of our self.

We can redefine how we create success in leadership.
We can define it as an unbounded expression of the feminine heart.
We can define it as our full capacity to stand in our excellence.
And tap into the realms of the inspired and the creative
and the innovative.
We can define it as the power to rise individually AND collectively in
our passions, purpose, prosperity and impact.

EVERY WOMAN CAN ACCESS THE ESSENTIAL POWERS OF THE FEMININE HEART.

Every woman embodies a range of feminine energies – powers of the feminine heart – within herself. Whilst these energies are alive within us, we can often find that one or more is dominant and it is within our dominant power that we can find our greatest strengths and skills. We can also find one of the essential powers is more prevalent at certain ages and stages of our lives. When a woman activates and loves all aspects of her essential power, she can rise up wholly and completely in her radiant, strong and beautiful feminine heart.

We can begin to nurture feminine values by
noticing how we live them.

How can we begin to nurture more of our feminine values? We can begin by taking a moment every day to notice how we live them. Look through the feminine values in the list below. Think of one value you'd like to encourage and enhance. Then, make a mental note of the action you'll take that day to embody and implement it. This is important because it is in daily life – during the times where you apply self-awareness – that real and lasting healing and change can take place.

At night, before you go to bed, reflect on your day to see how you lived that value.

And, even more importantly, explore how doing so made you feel.

FEMININE VALUES

» Connectedness. Wholeheartedness.

» Humility, listening, learning from others and sharing credit.

» Candor, a willingness to speak openly and honestly.

» Patience, a recognition that some solutions emerge slowly.

» Empathy, sensitivity to others that promotes

understanding.

» Trustworthiness, a track record and strength that inspires confidence.

» Openness, being receptive to the ideas and concepts of others.

» Flexibility, the ability to change and adapt when circumstances require.

» Vulnerability, the courage to make mistakes.

» Balance, sense of purpose.

» Being articulate, expressing clearly.

» Being dependable.

» Helpfulness, flexibility, and cooperation.

A few additional include:

» Intuitive

» Sincerity

» Kindness, compassion

» Generosity, giving

» Honesty

» Nurturance, caring

» Empathy

As you reflect on this list of values, it is easy to see that the feminine heart is the source of true power, intelligence, insight and understanding. Tap into this power and you can access the ability to transform your views of money and success, happiness and fulfillment – you unlock hidden talents, uncover new meaning and amplify the significance of your purpose.

In essence, accessing the power of the feminine heart moves you beyond old, outdated concepts about your capacities to create and to lead – becoming less about rules and expectations; and more about expressing your authentic voice, at home and at work.

How can you activate the essential powers of the feminine heart?

» **Openness.** A mastery of the feminine heart is found in being spontaneous and receptive to new ideas, open to hearing new thoughts, and surrendering to new ways of accomplishing. In this one shift into openness – be it with the voice of your intuition OR in your relationship with others – your relationship with the feminine heart will be magnified.

» **Inclusiveness.** Reach out to include or invite a person into your group and make them feel welcome. *Adopting an attitude of* warmth, genuine caring and acceptance is symbolic of the feminine heart in action.

» **Vulnerability.** The more you anchor into the

qualities of self-trust and self-loyalty, the easier it becomes to set free your authentic expression. Admitting you don't have all the answers and showing humility when you make a mistake: these are qualities often viewed as feminine traits. But, the fact is they project strength and confidence in a way that's beneficial for anyone.

» ***Friendship.*** *Offering* support, encouragement and being a nurturing friend is a feminine quality that is too often neglected in relationships. But when we are a supportive presence in anyone's life, the experience can be life changing for you, as well as the other person.

» ***Compassion.*** The ability to understand what others are feeling — to detect if they are overworked or frustrated — is a capacity that clearly contributes to empowered leadership. Loving kindness, the cornerstone of compassion, flows from values such as empathy, acceptance, and non-judgment. Being easy with yourself and deciding to put an end to your own self-judgment are expressions of loving-kindness. The same is true when you extend this attitude to others. Valuing employees as people, rather than vehicles for specific tasks is a trait that comes naturally to most female leaders. That's why women are known for building strong professional relationships. As honorable as compassion sounds, it simply comes down to deciding that you stand on the side of acceptance, rather than harsh judgment.

» ***Collaboration.*** There is power in collaboration. Moving from the isolated "I" to 'we" gives way to the power of creative diversity. Commit to surround yourself with people who can genuinely see you – those who value your talents – recognize your creative capacities. Then, design ways to support one another. The fact is a collaboration of different kinds of skills is what allows ideas, individuals, and businesses to thrive. If you want to continue to evolve, learn and grow, you have to be able to connect and collaborate with others who have different skill sets, experiences and perspectives.

» ***Wholeheartedness.*** The feminine heart thrives by pouring out love and appreciation. We see others as courageous when they speak up and speak out, yet we hold ourselves back out of fear and shame. These qualities are so alive and ready to flow into the world, yet many are hiding their beauty in fear of 'not being good enough,' or of being 'too much' if they let their love shine. The evolved feminine embraces the fullness of life and is loving, feeling, creative, spontaneous, devotional, and at times, fiercely inspiring. Commit to yourself to notice the times when you are most connected to these qualities.

» ***Inspiration.*** Find ways to invite more joy into your life by living from the source. Every day can be steeped in a flow of renewal. The opposite of renewal is habit, routine, mental conditioning, and fixed beliefs. So rather than struggling to be more inspired, use your efforts to remove the obstacles that block inspiration. Once you stop identifying with habit and routine, inspiration returns naturally.

» **Curiosity.** Curiosity is a vulnerable place to be. It requires living in the unknown, being uncertain, and allowing for new learning. A highly underestimated power, curiosity requires patience, stillness, and presence. In curiosity, a transformation is allowed to occur. When you suspend final judgment and watch with curiosity, something new is being formed. Planning is a very effective masculine tool. However, without the feminine principle of curiosity planning loses power. And without a healthy masculine energy, curiosity can flail and seem like indecision and chaos. Curiosity allows a plan or intention to evolve to a higher level of itself, as more information is revealed. Being open to new insight is a fundamental asset in both business and in life. The evolving feminine leaders who will succeed in the future are those who have a hunger for learning, driven by curiosity, that moves them to leave no stone unturned.

» *Deep Listening.* **Wonder what is beneath the surface?** Deep listening is a process of listening to learn. It requires the temporary suspension of judgment, and a willingness to receive new information – listening for understanding, rather than agreement – being open beyond one's preconceptions or assumptions.

» *Know What You Stand For.* Commit wholeheartedly to be a woman who stands strong for creating from the core of her true worth – to feel a sense of connection while you get things done – to accomplish what is meaningful and create the transformation you know you can make. A commitment to own your worth and value is the foundation for real and lasting shifts in your relationship with the essential powers of your feminine heart.

As you see the feminine heart in action, you will start to perceive more of its presence throughout your life. Getting more acquainted with each of the qualities, along with each of the essential powers, also means you can start to see how your feminine heart is already playing a significant role in your life, perhaps in surprising or unexpected ways. In contrast, you may also discover areas in your life where the feminine heart is void – identifying these areas will empower you to create the changes you desire.

It's important that we look for the feminine heart in action.
And, how those actions impact our lives.

HOW CAN YOU SPOT THE FEMININE HEART IN ACTION?

Rather than suppress or deny the qualities of the feminine heart, simply because the current culture may view them as less valuable, commit to amplifying those qualities, both personally and professionally. Recognize the qualities as a source of authentic power – a power that comes from the core of your true worth, steeped in the capacity to get things done, and accomplish what is meaningful.

Some of the qualities you might spot in action include:

» **Nurturance.** This quality of the feminine heart is active in a woman as she is called to give life to everything she touches. It can be giving birth to a creative idea or a new business. It can be giving life to those who need support or re-igniting a vision that is starting to stall or go stale. At the foundation of nurturance, we find the highest forms of creativity.

» **Advocacy.** Imagine a fierce 'mama bear' and you touch the qualities of the purest form of advocacy. Caregiving is advocacy. And in my opinion, some of the best leaders are caregivers. Advocacy and caregiving have traditionally been viewed as a feminine quality because it's associated with mothering. When we bring caregiving into business or the workplace, we find a leader who nurtures talents and inspires the best kind of work environment steeped in values, purpose and passion – care and support, allowing teams, colleagues, partners and associates to be their best.

» **Creative Intelligence.** At its foundation, creative intelligence involves going beyond what is given to generate novel and interesting ideas. This has always been one of the most necessary qualities and is called upon when innovation is needed. Thoughtful and observant, using both knowledge and intuition, creative intelligence is the quality that amplifies your abilities to easily discern and know the right thing is to do.

» **Community.** It is all about bringing people together in respect, creating a sense of belonging. Be it business teams or wanting to create a creative environment for yourself or others, being part of a community is an essential power for amplifying the strengths of the feminine heart. And a strong feminine heart makes for stronger families, stronger communities, stronger companies, stronger leaders, stronger ideas, and stronger solutions.

BEFORE YOU GET STARTED.

As you begin your study of *The Eight Essential Powers of the Feminine Heart*, the most important thing to remember is this is your own personal experience. The definition of what you consider to be an empowered feminine --- or the ways you individualize or connect with the powers of the feminine heart – is going to be different for everyone. It is a unique, individual path.

Some of what I do believe you and something that has long been my own thesis is that success in leadership is far more effective as we bring more of our feminine heart into a greater balance.

Here are five practices to support you in gaining greater value by bringing greater balance into your experience with this book:

Be willing to feel your feelings. Too often we expend enormous energy running away from our feelings. And too often, emotional connection and release is often interpreted as weak, purposeless, or diminishing.

A disconnection from the feminine heart can be experienced as a disconnection to emotions. To unlock our full creative capacities we need to access, fully feel and release emotion without harsh judgment. Otherwise, the feelings become locked in our physical body, blocking the flow of our energies.

As you begin to allow yourself to fully feel your feelings without judgment, the essential powers of the feminine heart can flow freely. Remember, loving acceptance begins with self-acceptance.

Set aside sacred time. Gift yourself sacred time to experience the material in this book. Sacred time is defined as your willingness to give yourself the space to move through the pages at your own pace. This will also create the space for your intuition to speak and be heard. Intuition is the voice of your feminine heart. And in order to fully access it, you must be in strong connection with your 'feeling body' – the flow of your emotions. Setting aside sacred time will allow you to define and/or redefine your relationship with the powers of the feminine heart. As well, discern the shifts you know you must make.

Dedicate yourself to trust. Trusting inner guidance, received as you explore the essential powers of the feminine heart, can sometimes take you out of your comfort zone. When your feminine heart begins awakening, there will likely be feelings of heightened energy. Very often you will feel restless or find your mind overcrowded with passing thoughts or distracted by things you need to do. These are all signs your feminine heart is stirring. Devote yourself to trust what you feel and any new insights that arise.

Create your own sacred space. The energy of the feminine heart is amplified by attention to aesthetics and your environment. It naturally responds to beautiful spaces that have been created with love and intention.

From lighting a candle to setting the tone for your study by repeating one of the I AM RISING intentional statements you'll find in Chapter Nine of this book – or in creating your own I AM RISING intentional statement – you are calling forth a connection with your feminine heart.

The important thing to keep in mind is that this is your own sacred space. Over time it will become imbued with the supportive energies of the feminine heart and will have a powerful effect on your consciousness.

Cultivate stillness. Dedicating time to cultivating stillness and quiet time for contemplation is vital for activating the powers of the feminine heart. It is challenging to amplify your inner-awareness and move through necessary change if you never create spaces of stillness, silence or reverence.

Stillness is not always a totally still body or sitting in silent meditation. It can be a walk in natural surroundings, with the intention of connecting to the feminine heart. It can be listening to inspirational music.

The key is that cultivating stillness becomes a regular practice; it is the process and regularity that over time creates the strengthening within. You will discover a rich well of abundant resources inside your stillness.

Let's get ourselves creating from a place where we're most enlivened, aligned, and empowered.

As you take steps to move forward, something to consider is, while feminine qualities are gaining greater praise, this does not mean our masculine nature needs to be shunned in an attempt to bring in more power for female energy.

The fact is, we can become both highly focused *and* caring. We can be nurturing while maintaining high standards of excellence. We are blazing a new trail of living into the powers of the feminine heart. And as part of this trailblazing, we are collectively developing a new paradigm of *feminine leadership* and *feminine success*, one that encourages, collaborates, praises, values and respects.

Something that we as amazing women leaders instinctively do exceedingly well.

Rise, Amazing Woman, Rise!

Marsh Engle

Within the feminine heart are the powers of a new style of leadership — powers that reflect the pure creative potential in each of us.

Questing into the dimensions of the feminine heart is an adventure that bring you to understand and grasp your gift to the world and that is *your highest acceptance of the amazing woman you are.*

There is nothing you can do that's more important than being self-realized — to truly know who you are, all of your creative capacities, all you stand for.

It is with this realization you become a beacon.

You become a symbol. Transcendent. Embodied.

In this way you will find, live, and become a reflection of your own personal legacy.

CHAPTER ONE

THE ESSENTIAL POWER TO EVOLVE

Written by Theresa Wray, Psy.D.

"When we evolve together, we rise above the predefined cultural conditioning that would have us playing small and silent. We rise above the negative chatter by focusing our intentions on bringing more love and light into the world.

And today, the world needs to hear our voices that can soften perspectives and lift us all up with love and compassion."

Theresa Wray

THE ESSENTIAL POWER TO EVOLVE

Are you listening to your own heart?

Evolving is the freeing process of letting go of the false beliefs and prescribed definitions that keep you playing small and silent. It's about rising up into your truth and writing your own story. It's about rising up into the power of your heart and sharing your unique gifts of love and compassion with the world.

When you're not living in your truth, you are not truly living and the world is missing your valuable contribution. I know this because this used to be my story until I found the courage to change it.

Have you ever been afraid to tell someone what you were really feeling for fear of being judged or rejected? I have.

I learned how to be silent and adapt to any role that people defined for me in exchange for safety, love and acceptance. I learned to stay stuck in the story they had written for me. I learned how not to evolve.

In the foster care system, I was praised for my ability to adapt to any role within a family. I helped people find the positive in negative situations and become valued as the peacemaker and problem solver. But for me, those were just tools in my survivor's kit. I carried my toolkit into adulthood. As long as everyone was happy, I knew I would be safe. Until one day, being safe wasn't enough.

Have you ever had a pivotal moment that shifted you to a new way of thinking and being, and you knew your life would never be the same? I have.

I didn't recognize the voice at first. It had been more than twenty years since I had heard from my big sister. Seeing each other gave life to the shame and fear that was anchored in our haunting past. She told me I had been on her bucket list for a few years. Now, she was in stage four cancer and afraid to let go of a life she had not yet fully lived.

For the next six months, our conversations unearthed the buried wounds as we embarked upon our spiritual, healing journey. She struggled to see her value. She was stuck in a story that someone else had written for her. I reminded her that she had adopted two children from the foster care system and had given them a loving home. But no matter what you do, when you are living inside someone else' definition, you will only value what they value. You will only believe what they believe. Together, we uncovered the lies we believed about ourselves. We laughed, cried and prayed, reconnected and rediscovered our truth.

When I received the call that she had passed, her husband said she was more alive in the past six months than she had ever been. She had rediscovered her voice through sketches that she had drawn over the years, reflecting her loving, abundant life. It occurred to her that each sketch told a story of what she had contributed and learned along her journey. As her life revealed itself to her, she told me that her greatest gift of all was the power of unconditional love that she had learned to give to herself and others.

In one of our last conversations, she said she would draw a sketch for me of birds flying in a vast, beautiful blue sky. The caption would read, "I am ready to soar."

She never drew that sketch, but she lived it. And as her spirit soared, she left behind in its wake an abundance of love and light. I realized my sister had evolved into the power of her own heart. Now, it was my turn. I learned that the first step in the process of evolving is to get unstuck.

We are all on this journey together, learning and growing as we pass through each other's lives. I am blessed with amazing compassionate friends. They've helped me learn to trust my own true voice and deliver it in a loving way through lessons of forgiveness and atonement. This was not an easy journey and I made mistakes along the way that served as beacons of light illuminating my path forward.

As I learned to read off script, most people who knew my true heart congratulated me for finally showing up. However, I did discover a few relationships that could not exist, unless I continued to live inside their definition of me. But their definition was based on their judgment of a past that was no longer a part of my story. I no longer served a purpose in their lives. I could no longer play small and silent. As soon as the doors closed, I realized that this was part of my journey. I was getting unstuck, but I still had work to do if I were to evolve.

As painful as it was to let go, I learned that the hurt only lives inside the mind. Evolving is the freeing process of letting go of false beliefs, and as we move into our truth we seek to listen and speak through our hearts in words of love and compassion. We are always evolving when our hearts are open to learning and giving. We continue to get stuck and unstuck, and we continue to evolve after each lesson. After much work on forgiveness and atonement, I was able to find a path to genuine love and gratitude. I blessed everyone along my journey and was grateful for the lessons I had learned. Like my sister, the most important lesson of all was the power of unconditional love that I learned to give to myself and others.

I believe God gives us exactly what we need in every moment. For every door that closed, new ones opened, revealing a meaningful life that was more aligned with my spirit. It's not easy getting unstuck from false beliefs. But once you do, you can't help but evolve into your truth. Doors will open. God or whatever words you choose to describe that universal force, will present the opportunities that were designed just for you when you are ready to walk into the life you were meant to live.

Have you ever had a moment of bravery when you said, "yes" to something and as soon as you were ready to do it, you wanted to run and hide? I have.

When I was asked to write this chapter, I heard myself say, "yes," but I also heard another voice. It was fear telling me that if I told you my true story, you would judge me and then reject me. But I know that many of you are a lot like me. We all get stuck. But when you are called to rise into your truth, it's for a higher purpose. It is because your story is needed at that time to heal yourself and others. We are all designed to love each other and support the unique gifts that we bring into the world. Fear doesn't stand a chance when we stand together in our love. The only way we can support each other is to discover the power within our own feminine hearts.

Inside the feminine heart beats a powerful capacity for love and compassion. We can use that power in positive ways, but first we must find it within ourselves. That's what evolving is all about. When we learn to love ourselves, we release a powerful, loving light that illuminates the dark areas of our lives and the lives of others. When we see each other with our hearts, our perspective softens. We know that the perceived failures we see in others and ourselves are the results of our separation from our true selves. The heart's vision focuses on love and those positive emotions navigate us back to our truth during the dark storms of our lives. We learn the power of unconditional love, forgiveness and atonement. We go to that truly honest place deep within our souls where we cannot hide. As we bring ourselves back into our own truth, we can no longer be stuck inside the false definitions that once stopped us from trusting and giving the gift of our whole, unique selves to the world.

It is especially difficult for women to evolve into their truth because the world we live in does not tell the truth about us. When the synonyms used to define femininity were written, the authors ignored the courageous feminine voices that shook the societal percepts from their moral ground and made room for transformational change.

Still today, the same antiquated synonyms are used to reinforce the chasm between masculine and feminine traits. Feminine traits are considered weak within the societal structure. They are defined as empathic, expressive, and sensitive, to name a few. In businesses, women leaders are described as leading emotionally from the heart, as if they are devoid of the intellectual, reasoning mind. But these definitions of the feminine heart do not tell our true story.

Organizations, the political arena and other models of success in the Western culture have been traditionally based on masculine traits. The definitions of women support the systematic socialization that has kept us small and silent in our homes, in our relationships, and in the world. It's time for all of us to reclaim and honor the power of the feminine heart. The seeds have already been planted, the landscape has already been cultivated, and our evolution is ripe for transformation right now.

When women rise, they are like ripples in the water, constantly evolving as they reshape the landscape of the feminine culture.

The chasm in the bedrock of the gender culture is beginning to narrow. Today, organizations are discovering the strengths inherent in the feminine traits of empathy and compassion. Men, as well as women, are slowly becoming liberated from their gender roles as they share the power of these collective human traits.

Like a tightly stitched tapestry, we have been carefully knitted together into the fabric of this predefined gender culture. The unraveling of these antiquated gender ideas began many years ago when amazing women throughout generations began to rise up and speak out against the issues of their time.

For example, women like Sojourner Truth, Susan B. Anthony, Elizabeth Cade Stanton, and Ida B. Wells, began to weave a new, colorful, all-inclusive tapestry of humanity. These brave, amazing women, along with many others, rose up into their truth and introduced a new way of thinking, behaving and being in the world. As a result, new laws were created that transformed societal norms and opened doors for all women to lend their voices as leaders, educators and healers.

When Dr. Gertrude Elion won the Nobel Prize in medicine in 1988 for developing the AIDS drug, AZT and other drug treatments, she said, "In my day they said that women don't do chemistry. I saw no reason why we couldn't." She listened to her own voice, followed her own passion as a healer and saved millions of lives.

The list of amazing, powerful women throughout our history is long. But you don't have to be a Noble Prize winner to make a big difference. Rachel Platten sings in her "Fight Song" about how one small boat on the ocean can put big waves into motion. That is true for all of us. We are each specially designed with our own unique gifts to be included in that beautiful, colorful tapestry of humanity. Without you, there is a valuable and much-needed piece missing.

All of us amazing women have one thing in common. We made a commitment to rise in the midst of adversity and stand tall in our truth. And we are not alone. We stand on the shoulders of great women who stood bravely before us and positively influenced our lives. My mother was one of those brave women whom no one ever thought could rise, until she did.

She was a single mother struggling with a critical illness when she began to rise up and live her truth. She refused to play the victim. The taboo of being a weak, divorced woman did not define her. That was not her story.

When the doctors told her she would not live another day, she lived another year helping terminally ill children find their voices through drawings and stories they had written together. They said it couldn't be done, but soon that children's wing was transformed into a creative space filled with life as volunteers continued her work with many amazing children.

She instilled in me a positive, optimistic view of the world. I watched her survive adversities and find within them opportunities from which to thrive. She found the positive light in the midst of the dark storms in her life and showed others how to access this power within themselves. She celebrated the lessons she had learned along her journey and passed them along to help others succeed. She rewrote her story and softened the rough edges of life with the power of her feminine heart.

My mother passed the torch to her amazing daughters. It used to feel arrogant to say that, but the old shame game was drowned out by my mother's voice. She believed that if you were not giving your gifts and learning experiences back to the world, then they are meaningless.

With my mother's message in mind, I was inspired to complete my doctoral program in psychology with an emphasis in organizational management and consulting. I wanted to understand human behavior and the positive principles that my mother embodied. Where did they come from? How did she use them to not only overcome adversity, but to expand her own capacity to help others move forward in a positive way? My heart was stirring and a vision was beginning to form. I wanted to understand how I could use these principles to build employee's strengths and positive organizational cultures, to support sharing communities and to heal individual hearts.

My growing passion to deliver this meaningful service back to the world led me to renowned life coach, Tony Robbins and the Robbins-Madanes Coaching Program. As I studied life coaching and other spiritual teachings, I began to recognize the amazing woman emerging from within. For the first time ever, I began to value my education. I began to value and understand my mother's life principles and their positive impact on other's lives. I began to value and trust my own life's wisdom that, combined with all that I had learned, led me to the creation of Power Life Synergy™, my signature work and contribution.

Power Life Synergy™ is a system that uses the five dimensions of the human spirit that empowered my life's experiences and brought my mother's principles to life. Together, they are synergistically used to drive Awareness, Alignment and Action to the whole-person experience in careers, relationships and unique contributions to the world. This synergistic journey emulates my personal evolution. It's about letting go of false beliefs and learning positive shifts that reveal the strengths of your true spirit. It's about living in your truth and contributing your gifts of joy, love and passion as you evolve into the power of your heart.

We can all live our passion when we make a commitment to live the authentic life that we were born to live. Every feminine heart has a calling and a powerful voice from which to respond. Once I got unstuck from other people's judgment and definitions of me, I saw my own heart very clearly and rose up into a loving space deep within my soul where I could hear my own heart's voice.

Are you listening to your own heart? Are you ready to rise up and evolve into it?

It's hard to hear your heart over the noise of other people's voices telling you who we are and who you are not. The ego speaks so much louder than the soft tones of our souls. We were not born to spin around in someone's ego or our own. We were born to be vessels of love and light. This special love and light that you give to the world is generated from your own heart.

How do we rise together and allow the power of our unique and beautiful hearts to overflow into the world?

I think it's important when we talk about evolving collectively to understand that it starts with you. Together, we can make a transformational difference in the world when we connect one evolving heart with another.

I'm telling you my story unashamedly and unapologetically because I know you are a lot like me. It's easy to stay stuck in the ego mind or someone else's definition of us and to not evolve into our truth. Until one day you know that if you don't evolve, your spirit and all the gifts that lie within it will become extinct.

There comes a time when the needs of the world are so great that it calls deeply to all of us. There is a calling for the passion locked in your heart right now. It takes all of us to heal the broken areas of this world. Now is the time to address the issues in our society, our government, within our communities and within our own homes. Once you start, there is no stopping the momentum. When we, the amazing women of our generation rise together, we can make positive, transformational changes around the globe and within individual hearts. But it starts with you, one individual heart at a time making that personal commitment to live your passion and give your truth to the world.

What is your story? How are you evolving the power of your feminine heart?

It's time to add your own unique special colors to this beautiful tapestry of humanity. We can all make a difference and nobody's gifts are more important than another's. This world needs all of us. We are all on this journey together and we can learn from each other when we listen and see each other with our hearts.

When we evolve together, we rise above the pre-defined cultural conditioning that would have us playing small and silent. We rise above the negative chatter by focusing our intentions on bringing more love and light into the world. And today, the world needs to hear our voices that can soften perspectives and lift us all up with love and compassion.

Now, it's your turn. Rise, Amazing Woman, Rise! Write your own story. Let the world hear your voice and feel the power of your unique feminine heart!

THERESA WRAY

Theresa Wray holds a Doctorate in Psychology and Organizational Management. She is an inspirational life coach, a motivational speaker, teacher, author and a Human Resources Business Consultant. She is the creator of POWER Life Synergy™; a system that aligns five dimensions of the human spirit to drive Awareness, Alignment, and Action into the whole-person experience at work, in relationships and in their contributions to the world. Theresa inspires and motivates others by providing a safe exploratory space for people to transform their strengths, love, and joy into meaningful experiences in their work and personal lives. Learn more about Theresa Wray and her work by visiting www.PowerLifeSynergy.com.

CHAPTER TWO

THE ESSENTIAL POWER OF SELF-LOVE

Written by Pamela Nebeker

"There are times in our lives where a revolution of the soul brings the revelations needed to guide us back to self-love. A revolution of the soul can look like a crisis: the end of a marriage, the death of a child or partner, or even life-threatening illnesses.

Our soul is calling us to awaken. And so, it begins one revelation at a time. Beginning with one act of self-love at a time. Line upon line, at every age, though the beauty of self-love we begin to rise."

Pamela Nebeker

THE ESSENTIAL POWER OF SELF-LOVE

Can beauty be magnified through self-love?

Self-love is offering the same kindness to ourselves that we offer to a stranger. It is seeing the beauty in every situation and every person. When you love yourself, you glow from the inside out. Whether you are a Maiden, a Mother, or a Monarch, self-love will illuminate your life. It will help you attract your tribe, those who resonate with your dreams, and those who respect and love you for who you are. Everything starts with how you feel about yourself. Start feeling worthy, brilliant, and beautiful. Be willing to receive all that this life has to offer.

Every great teacher has weighed in on self-love. In the New Testament in the book of Mathew, 22:34-40, Jesus tells us to love God with all our hearts and to love our neighbor as our self. Buddha teaches that you must love The Self before extending unconditional love. Self-love and compassion are qualities of your divine nature. The Torah teaches us to love our fellow as our self. Islam teaches it is imperative to love one's self in order to love others.

We come into this world with love, awe, honesty, excitement for life, and the ability to learning. Gradually we relinquish these through our choices, cultural experiences, and sometimes well-meaning family, friends, and teachers at church or school.

How do we practice self-love when our sense of self is broken and our sense of belonging has been compromised?

Our mothers and grandmothers did the very best they could. Sometimes they were limited in their capacity or circumstance to show us the maternal love that we all need to get started. This can lead to a sense of not belonging and a deep, heartbreaking loneliness. You are not alone, and I promise you that there are other ways to find that maternal love and nurturing that may have eluded you and kept you from learning self-love. By healing ourselves through self-love, we can change things for our children, our children's children, and our mothers and grandmothers. In this healing, we all rise. Our mothers and grandmothers are freed from the burdens that they were unable to define and heal. Our children will rise to be better parents, better human beings, and even better citizens of this world.

Many of us create a False Self as we grow up. Sometimes we lose ourselves in marriage or divorce as young mothers, or perhaps we feel hopeless and without value as we age. The beauty of this awareness is that we can change it. We can find ourselves and love ourselves again. We can begin again. As we implement self-love into our lives, we meet our authentic selves.

The universe has a way of providing exactly what and who we need to show us the way. Throughout my life, I found role models in women who nurtured themselves and others. As early as elementary school I began identifying them. One of the first women was a classmate's mother. She was lovely, a hard worker, and an amazing horticulturist. Everything she grew was lush, healthy, and bountiful. Her gift for arranging flowers was poetic, but her real gift was how she made me feel about myself. She always had a kind uplifting word and treated me as an equal. Another woman was my high school art teacher. She knew how to care for herself. She was bold, gorgeous, and shared great wisdom. Her best advice to me was, "Get out of Dodge right after graduation." I listened and began a great adventure two thousand miles away from home. My art teacher spent her life being a mothering influence for hundreds, if not thousands, of young girls. Women like these set the example of nurturing in positive ways. They had healthy boundaries and were strong.

God has always sent the angels I've needed. We must open our eyes, ears, hearts, and minds to see them. As a child, they showed up as neighbors, teachers, parents of friends, and in books. All of them were imperfect, but perfect for me.

Later as a mother of small children, my vision of anything beyond that was non-existent. You might say I was in the thick of what I had always imagined to be my life purpose. Life has a way of bringing up our fears so we face them. Suddenly, I was divorced for the second time at forty. I was scared I would end up alone, sitting in a chair for the next forty years just like my grandma did after my Grandpa passed on. Her body became molded to the shape of that chair. She quit living and just existed. This image had me scared half to death. One day, out of the blue, a wise friend gave me a precious gift: a black and white photo of a stunning, incandescent woman in her late fifties. This photo became my vision for the future. Having no idea who she was, I simply embraced her as family and hung her in my hall gallery with the faces of my beloved children. Her dynamic, radically honest, all-knowing presence somehow gave me great hope. Over time, she became my silent teacher. It was there in her quiet radiance that I began to recognize my own self. I allowed her silence to guild me to become a confident, radiant, inspired woman. She gave me hope for my future. We all need mentors to guide us into every chapter of our lives.

Gradually I stopped fighting growing older and began aging into beauty. I let my hair turn silver and white, and grew it long and wild down my back. Wrinkles became the precious evidence that I had lived with courage, labored with might, and laughed with joy. Finally, instead of feeling like a lost cause, I began taking up a cause: my cause. I found authenticity in who I am and embraced our cause of changing the way we think about growing older.

Angels show up in many ways to help us understand that we are loved and that there is hope for all of us. Some angels are alive, some are heavenly, and some are seeds sown into the fabric of our souls, left waiting to be awakened. Let the revelations begin.

Revelation is the Revolution of the Soul.

There are times in our lives where a revolution of the soul brings the revelations needed to guide us back to self-love. A revolution of the soul can look like a crisis, the end of a marriage, the death of a child or partner, or even life-threatening illnesses. Our soul is calling us to awaken. And so, it begins one revelation at a time. Beginning with one act of self-love at a time. Line upon line, though love we begin to rise.

REVELATIONS OF SELF-LOVE #1
The feeding of one's spirit begins with gratitude

My journey back to loving myself began when I was thirty-four, a divorced mother with six children between the ages of five months and eight years old. I came upon a book that changed my life called "Simple Abundance: A Daybook of Comfort and Joy," by Sarah Ban Breathnach. I will forever be grateful to her. This was my new beginning, my introduction to the power of gratitude, and my new awareness into seeing the beauty that was all around me. My eyes began to open to a brighter present, filled with awe, beauty, and newfound hope for the future. This was my first revelation in a very long time with many more to come. Line upon line, precept upon precept, we learn to love ourselves as God loves us.

The opportunities for self-love are forever unfolding. It's not one big revelation as much as it is a series of small revelations that begin to enlighten and awaken the soul. It's noticing the red geraniums against the ocher-yellow house that you have driven past hundreds of times. It's the sound of children's laughter as your ears awaken and take notice. It's the feeling of moss under your bare feet as they kiss the earth, grounding you to this magical world. It's the smell of fall leaves, bonfires, and hot apple cider. It's the taste of local honey drizzled on warm, homemade bread. It's that still, small voice that begins to rumble inside you, speaking from your authentic self. That is the revelation that erupts from the revolution of the soul. Self-love is the awakening of all the senses. Self-love begins with gratitude.

REVELATION OF SELF-LOVE #2

Comfort soothes the soul

Just as a baby needs soothing, so do we. We have a tendency to forget this because life is full of responsibilities, jobs, relationships, and stressful demands. Many of us choose to self-medicate, which is the opposite of self-soothing. There are better ways. This is one way I found mine.

My curiosity of cultures, religions, and sacred rituals lead me to Feng Shui. I read every book I could get my hands on. I studied with a Master and became a certified Feng Shui consultant. It was really a quest to help myself, but then my experience became a way to help others. It was on this journey that I discovered a new way to create vision boards using the BAU GUA, THE CIRCLE OF LIFE. The elements of the earth called to me to balance my life. Part of the course included a personality test. I scored high in the fire, wood, and earth elements. I lived for growth, passion, and expansion, but I was lacking in water and metal energies. Water represents calmness, retrospect, and rebirth. Metal represents strength and discipline.

I began by spending more time with water. We happened to have purchased a fixer-upper with a 1950's kidney-shaped pool. The renovation came to a screeching halt when my second husband decided he no longer wanted to be married. That pool was my saving grace. Cleaning it became my meditation in the early hours before the kids got up. During my divorce, that water helped heal my broken heart. I pulled a cushion next to the edge and laid there listening to the calming sounds of the water lapping back and forth. When fall arrived, I turned up the heater and continued to swim at night after the kids went to sleep. The earth elements have a way of soothing us.

We find ways to self-soothe through self-care, healthy food, music, continued education, movement, and finding joy in this beautiful planet and those we love.

Whether it's hiking, biking, walking on the beach, or putting our feet in the soil while planting our spring gardens, Mother Earth has the power to soothe and heal.

REVELATION OF SELF-LOVE #3

Becoming the calm in life's storm by stilling the noise of the mind

My introduction to meditation was a Tibetan mantra about letting go and letting God in. I love that mantra. (I still chant it often, especially in the shower).

"Gate, gate, paragate, parasamgate. Bodhi svaha."

Translation: Gone, gone, gone beyond. Oh, what an awakening.

Later I learned that many different things can be used as meditation: the simplicity of lighting a candle, the mundane chore of making a bed, the breathtaking beauty of the sunrise, or even the drizzle of rain. Hand washing the dishes is sacred, calming, and real.

One of my favorite fun meditations is to buy a bottle of kid's bubbles for blowing. I'll sit on my balcony, blow bubbles, and observe. Each is unique in size and shape. They dance as the wind carries them away, and I imagine my worries being carried away with them.

Another favorite meditation of mine is being in my garden feeling the breeze, the grass, and breathing in the fragrant flowers as if to become one with them. Getting my hands dirty in the earth has always been healing. Nature can be our best meditation. Some Japanese doctors prescribe a forest walk to help still the minds of those suffering from anxiety and depression. Trees can bring such an overwhelming sense of calm to all of our senses.

When we take time to breathe in beauty, we experience stillness. It's as though the mind slows down. It helps us be and live in the present moment more often. I have a favorite shop in Salt Lake City called "Ward and Child Garden Store." It's my feel-good place. Just walking in the door washes peace over me. I've had the privilege of introducing my clients to this magical place. It is truly a blissful experience. There is a glorious secret garden in the back that is a perfect place to find the peace one longs for in this world.

Meditation calms my soul and replaces jumbled nerves with a connection to self and to God. Many things are meditations, including bubbles, gardens, and doing the dishes. As we begin to see beauty in every person, every task, and every situation in our lives, then and only then do we become one with God, ourselves, and each other.

Heal thyself and we heal the world.

In closing, it is only through a sense of belonging and through a series of profound revelations that we can allow ourselves to fully experience self-love. It begins with gratitude, awareness, and connection. People can inspire us and love us unconditionally, but they cannot give us the love that only we can give ourselves. The late Maya Angelo once said, "If I am not good to myself, how can I expect anyone else to be good to me?" It took me a long time to learn to be good to me.

Self-love is seeing the beauty in every person and every situation.

One revelation at a time, line by line, we allow the awakening to begin. This is true in every time of our lives. We begin as a Maiden in our youth, we grow into a nurturing Mother, and we blossom in beauty and wisdom as the Monarch. Together we can uplift and mentor each other. Together we move each other out of the fear of aging and change the perspective that every age can be beautiful, glamorous, productive, and impactful. In this awakening, we begin to rise and help others to do the same.

PAMELA NEBEKER

Pamela Nebeker is a lover of beauty and a seeker of truth.

As a podcaster, speaker, and author, she teaches the power of embracing life at every age. Pamela is changing the way we think about growing old. She is the creator of *The Art of Age Now*, a movement that inspires women to be their best in every decade of their lives. She is married to the man of her dreams and lives in

Los Angeles, California. She has eight grown children and five beautiful grandchildren. Pamela invites you to join her on this courageous journey of aging into the beauty of who we truly are.

www.theartofagenow.com

www.pamelanebeker.com

CHAPTER THREE

THE ESSENTIAL POWER OF INTUITION

Written by Wendy L. Yost

"I allow myself to be guided in the direction of what I want to experience more of."

Wendy L. Yost

THE ESSENTIAL POWER OF INTUITION

What would you need to be willing to consistently trust
yourself and your senses -- including your intuition?

Our POWER of INTUITION can be an amazing guide in all aspects of our lives, if we let it. Yet, learning to listen and trust our intuition is not something we are taught. In fact, in most cultures, we are actively steered away from doing so, and encouraged to listen to outer authorities, instead of becoming our own.

What would become possible for you if you consistently felt connected and supported? If you were prepared to take your next step? If you had a vision for where you were headed – but didn't feel the need to control the details? If you felt attuned to signs, symbols and synchronicities? And if you felt naturally called to nurturing people, places and experiences?

With that much good available, what is it that gets in the way of experiencing and trusting our intuition on a more regular basis? From my own experience, and what I've observed with thousands of university students and coaching clients, three things hinder us: limiting its application, comparing ourselves to others and inviting distraction.

For much of humanity's existence, our instincts and intuition have been hardwired for our survival, alerting us to anything that might jeopardize our physical safety. This was hugely important when our life expectancies were 30-35 years. Yet, in our modern lives, while we are no longer under threat of attack by a lion, tiger, leopard or crocodile, an essential part of ourselves is still wired to respond as if it is. And one of the ways we can enhance our intuition and learn to trust it in new ways is by elevating and reassigning it to areas of our daily lives. We can put it to use in ways that exceed surviving and have us move toward greater thriving.

After reassigning the ways we apply our intuition, another barrier to its steady and trusted use is comparing our intuitive experiences to those shared by others. There are so many ways of knowing, and just because your ways of knowing differ from someone else's, doesn't make either way any less valid. We'll explore the most common. And we'll explore some lesser-known ways of knowing later in the chapter.

Say you take on consciously choosing to reassign your intuition the task of your thriving, in addition to surviving. And you are willing to accept that your ways of knowing are equally valid to other people's ways of knowing. One last barrier remains that can create a void of guidance where a wellspring would otherwise occur. And that is how we choose to distract ourselves. Intuition involves listening and listening involves focusing our attention on what we are listening to. And yet, *so much* is competing for our attention throughout a typical day. And some of it, we invite. Like the multiverse that is our cell phones. While you can use your phone to develop your intuition by downloading Meditation for Intuition Apps or listening to related Podcasts, and bookmarking websites for animal totems, more often than not, our phones take us out of the present moment. And the present moment is the delivery vehicle for intuition. This is why you may find that you get insights while drying your hair, taking a familiar scenic drive, or watching squirrels scamper about – some of your attention is on what you are doing, yet much of it remains available and receptive.

To get a sense of the state of *your* relationship to intuition, and how these possible barriers might be influencing your experience of your intuition, you can consider mapping your relationship with your intuition from birth until now.

When I did so, it brought a number of powerful insights that allowed me to befriend my intuition in new ways. The process is a simple one. Take a sheet of paper, start with the year you were born and then track how you have interacted with your intuition and how you have observed the intuition of others throughout the years – as a child, a teenager, a young adult and now as a grown woman. See if you can come up with a list of ten points of reference. You don't need to include a bunch of details, just a short phrase or sentence for each item that comes to mind. Try not to edit. Just write down what comes.

Once you have your *Top Ten List,* see if you can find any patterns or themes. Were there any repeated people, places or experiences mentioned that are worth noting? Were there times you ignored your intuition? What happened when you *did* follow it?

My *Top Ten List* illuminated key influences that impacted my relationship to intuition, such as, specific people who taught me about intuition and championed my listening to it, places that seemed to heighten my sense of intuition and most of all, experiences where guidance was received, I followed it and it made a huge difference. It also highlighted several times where I received guidance, didn't follow it, and something other than what I wanted to happen, happened.

Several of my best memories tended to involve my *slowing things down in the moment* to clear my mind about my options and what I wanted to have happen next. Then setting a positive intention. And my being open to options I might not have otherwise considered. For example, when I was 30 years old and I experienced a job search that took *much longer* than I had anticipated. I had left a job I knew was not a match and I thought that with a Master's Degree and seven years of professional experience it would be easy enough to find a new one. Worried by the volume of applications I was sending out and the lack of interviews coming my way, I was in a panic. My Mom assured me a better match would surface and suggested that, in the meantime, I focus on what I enjoyed doing when I was younger -- things like babysitting, pet sitting, house sitting and so on.

Unsure of the going rates for personal services of this sort, I sent an email to two former mentors and asked what they typically paid for people they hired to help with such things, along with a quick update on my job search. One encouragingly wrote back, "You're available?" She shared that her organization was in the process of writing a job description for a position that hadn't existed before and that she thought I would be a good candidate. I applied, was hired, and not only was my job search finally over, but the job I was hired into was a dream job for me at the time. From that experience, I learned that sometimes taking action, even in small ways, like doing more of what I already enjoyed, sent me down a path that provided needed income at the time, and also led to a conversation that resulted in my next job.

Being selected for a TED Talk provided another lesson in intuition and how some things are beyond our conscious ability to orchestrate. When I learned that the university where I teach, had secured a TED License and would be hosting a TED event, I was ecstatic! I immediately messaged the Event Curators inquiring about whether they had secured all the speakers needed for the inaugural event. I got a polite, yet generic, response back indicating that Speaker Applications would be made available in the coming weeks and to check back. Fast forward to a Saturday night, a week or so later, I am running errands in my neighborhood, and I see a former student standing on a street corner with a huge suitcase. I am on my way to a party across town, and the thought arises, "Offer Gio a ride." I had already passed him as the thought caught my attention, so I turned around, rolled down my window, and asked, "Need a ride?"

He was happy to see me, as was one of his friends named Jamie whom I had met previously. Also loading into my car was Ruby, another student from the university. Turns out Gio had been accepted into the University's Study Abroad Program, needed a new suitcase, and they were waiting to catch the next bus to a location near the party I was already headed to. What happened next still puts a smile on my face.

After getting the latest updates from Gio and Jamie, I asked Ruby about her Major and if she was involved in any Clubs or Organizations on campus. When she shared that she was in The Entrepreneur Club, I smiled, looked at her through the rear-view mirror, and (tried to) casually ask, "Isn't that the student organization that secured the TED License?" Before I could finish my sentence, Gio and Jamie excitedly announced that they thought I would be a great speaker. I shared I had inquired about whether speakers had been selected or not and was told to stay tuned. We arrived at their destination and when the three of them left my car, it felt like something significant had just been set in motion. On Monday, I got a new message from the Curators of TED CSUN. They wanted to meet me on Tuesday, and by the end of the week I was a confirmed speaker. I still shake my head in a sense of awe and wonder when I think about how that all came together.

And, it reminds me that a huge part of learning to trust our intuition comes from residing in the present moment and noticing what you notice. A bazillion things had to line up for the three of them to be where they were, while I was driving in the direction I was. My mind could have been elsewhere, and I would not have seen Gio. I could have heard the inner prompting to offer him a ride and ignored it, thinking I needed to get to the party I was heading to. And yet, I was present, I noticed what I noticed, the guidance came, and I followed it. And I now have an archived TED Talk, a 15-minute version of the leadership course that I've taught at California State University, Northridge for over a decade.

The final positive example I want to share from my Top Ten list included just two words: "change lanes." Of all the examples that I listed, this is the one that reminds me most of why learning about and learning to trust my intuition matters so much. I was traveling Northbound on one of the busiest freeways in Los Angeles. A few exits before the one I was planning to take, I heard within me, "change lanes." It wasn't a scary, screaming or panicked voice. It wasn't even a rushed voice. It was a slow and steady action step awaiting my acceptance of the invitation being offered. I changed lanes, not even really considering it, just doing it. And within a matter of seconds, the car that was behind me crashed into the car that was in front of me. Not a bad accident, as thankfully the traffic had us traveling at slower speeds, but enough of an accident where you know all involved will likely need car repairs that require insurance claims. My eyes must have been as big as saucers, and my heart was racing. I looked to ensure that everyone was okay and once I realized they were, I went about my day. I was kept safe because I didn't ignore the intuition or pause to analyze it. I simply took action.

In addition to looking at the times we got guidance, listened to it and took related action, I think it's also important to look at the times we got guidance, didn't listen to it and there were consequences. Not from a place of superstition or beating ourselves up over it. But from a place of realizing that an easier path forward was being offered, we declined it...*and we can do differently next time.*

Like the time I put my cell phone on the rear bumper of my car and immediately had the thought, "that's not a good place for that," got distracted, got in my car and pulled out of my driveway. It wasn't until I got to the nearest stoplight and reached for my phone that I remembered where I left it. Thankfully I was able to backtrack my steps and find it in my driveway, but it had fallen off the bumper and gotten crunched in the process. *Ugh.* I remember being mad about the phone that now needed repair. And even angrier with myself, knowing the situation could have been avoided, had I just listened to myself.

I encourage you to revisit your *Top Ten List* and see what comes to heart and mind. You might even take a centering breath and ask, "What more is there for me to know about this?" Be still and see what comes. If you're a writer, have a pen or keyboard handy. If you're an artist, a canvas. A dancer, room to move. Use your natural forms of expression as a way to help you see what might want to be healed and/or revealed through this exploration. If answers don't come immediately, ask again before bed for the answers to come to you in the form of memorable dreams. Through my work I've come to see that some insights, especially those with the power to transcend outdated beliefs and transform us, are often on time release -- parceled out as we become ready to receive them, and in ways that allow for easier integration.

Intuition is *not* one size fits all. Learning to explore your own experiences helps you develop your own inner library of guidance to pull from. Doing so before you start learning more about different facets of intuition can help you in discerning how intuition works naturally for you. Hopefully, you'll also get curious about the different ways you might expand upon how intuitive guidance comes to you.

If you conduct an online search for "Intuition" you will eventually come across something called, *"The Clairs."* And likely see definitions for the four primary "Clairs." See which ones feel most familiar:

Clairaudience – Clear Hearing

Perceiving sounds or words from sources broadcasting from the spiritual or ethereal realm.

Claircognizance – Clear Knowing

Knowing without explanation or reason.

Clairsentience – Clear Feeling

Acquiring knowledge by feeling.

Clairvoyance – Clear Seeing

Seeing objects, actions, or events without the use of your physical eyes.

You may also find lesser known, yet no less valid, "Clairs" that deliver guidance in additional ways:

Clairempathy – Clear Feeling of Emotion

Psychically experiencing the thoughts or attitudes of a person, place, or animal and feeling the associated mental, emotional, physical, and/or spiritual results.

Clairgustance - Clear tasting

Tasting something without actually putting it into your mouth.

Clairsalience – Clear Smelling

Smelling a fragrance or odor of something or someone not in one's surroundings.

Clairtangence – Clear Touching

Handling an object or touching something and in doing so, knowing information about the object, its owner or its history that was not known beforehand.

Finally, there are forms of intuition that exist, yet haven't until recently been described. I was excited to learn of these two, mentioned in a related online article by Emily Matweow:

Claireloquence – Clear Communicating

Using precisely the right word or combination of words in order to accomplish a specific objective.

Clairtaction – Intuitive Touch

Sensing that you are being touched by a spiritual being or entity and knowing of information about that spirit, as well as the ability to extend touch to both physical and etheric entities in such a way that all involved are aware of the feeling.

As you can see, our intuition has a lot of ways of communicating with us. And, just as I learned about the initial four, which led to learning about others – and most recently the final two listed above, I anticipate that in the future greater emphasis and trust will be put on intuition as a viable means for assessing our circumstances and taking guided action. As a result, we will continue to invent new ways to articulate our intuitive experiences.

Your intuition is uniquely your own. Some argue that you came into this life with an encoded Blue Print for all the ways your intuition is designed to work naturally. And now you know that these ways of listening can also be learned, refined over time and drawn upon situationally, like reaching for the right tool for the right task.

Something remarkable is made possible when we are willing to notice what you notice and see things in new ways. My hope is that the conversation you have with yourself, by creating your *Top Ten List,* is *just the beginning* of enhancing your relationship with your intuition and deepening your trust in it. And that as you deepen your relationship with your intuition in one way, it inspires curiosity in another. I know that has been my experience as I've come to explore an array of topics like: Crystals for Intuition, Divination Tools for Intuition, Essential Oils for Intuition, Flower Essences for Intuition, Meditations for Intuition, Nutrition for Intuition and Prayers for Intuition. In short, there are many ways we can enhance our intuition and curiosity is key.

You have something unique to offer the planet – you could be holding a piece of a puzzle that could be life-changing for yourself and others. There could be an innovation that you alone hold the key to. By exploring your power of intuition, and in getting curious about those aspects of intuition you are less familiar with, you can come to know yourself and your abilities in new ways. You are also positioned to live in more empowered ways and be of greater service. As new guidance flows to you, you will have a clearer sense of how to have it work *for you,* however you choose to relate to, use and appreciate it.

When we honor our intuition, we free up our energy because we are no longer or are less often, defaulting to try and control our circumstances or figure things out. Instead, we trust ourselves and the moment at hand and get curious about what is being offered through it. And I think that's something worth exploring, in new ways, every day.

Wendy L. Yost

Wendy L. Yost inspires intentional action by combining leadership and spiritual principles. Examples include her TED Talk and a series of Leadership Academies that she offers, based on a university leadership course that she has taught 35+ times over the last decade. Wendy has contributed chapters to several best-selling books and is currently working on a Children's Book to create conversations about trusting ourselves and our senses, including intuition. A common thread woven through all of Wendy's work is her passion for helping people reconfigure their thoughts and their lives, so they have more time, energy and attention for what matters most – and in working intuitively to assist people in seeing what is being made available amidst even the most trying of life's circumstances. To learn more about Wendy Yost and her work visit: www.moreisavailable.com.

CHAPTER FOUR

THE ESSENTIAL POWER OF PRESENCE

Written by Conni Ponturo

"Presence comes into our world when we are ready to stand still and be in our power. The power comes from being excited to live in this moment and allowing yourself to be within the moment and listen."

Conni Ponturo

THE ESSENTIAL POWER OF PRESENCE

The real question we must ask; how can I truly embody the elegance of being present to my own power?

Presence - Being aware and excited to be fully in the moment. Standing perfectly still, aware and content to be right where you are. Not looking ahead or behind, but standing still, that's where presence shows itself. Presence is your ability to stand bright and full in each moment.

Do you feel present in your life? Feet fully on the ground in every moment?

Or, do you feel like you are just going through the motions of life, everything passing you by, and suddenly, you pick your head up, and months or years have gone by?

I think I have some answers for you about all of this, and hopefully some steps that can help you become more aware of when you are dropping out of awareness, and a simple way to bring you back into presence.

What does it mean to be present?
1. It means you are awake in your life.
2. You are fully aware and connected to your body and the environment around you.
3. You notice what's around you and are open to opportunities.
4. You are in the truth of your body.
5. You are not looking behind or ahead.
6. You can stop and stand still.
7. Presence brings a sense of calmness and joy.

And, what does it when you are not present?
1. You are overthinking, over-stressing, and over-worrying.
2. You are projecting circumstances and "what-if's."

3. You worry about what you don't have, rather than focusing on what you do have.
4. You are spinning out of control.
5. You are not in your body.
6. You are not in your heart.
7. You are all in your head.

I began to see how "unpresent" I was in my life. The feeling came over me one day, and I can't really explain it, but I felt something was off, and I was in a fog. That's when it hit me...I was missing my life. I started to become quiet enough to hear the whispers in my heart, and I realized that I had reached a pivotal moment in my career. I knew I was going through the motions of my day and my teaching, and I needed to fully embody the work I was here to share.

I teach my clients to love their bodies and to treat them with respect and love, but was I really living that? Was I giving my own body the love and respect I needed? I also grappled with knowing there was a deeper meaning in my teaching. I didn't even know what I meant by that, but I felt it, and I had to allow myself to go with that feeling. I knew I had to allow myself to fall apart and take a more inward perspective through journaling, meditation, and contemplation to lift myself out of the fog. I began to put myself out there more in my community. I took better care of my body. I focused on being present in my conversations with friends and family, and I began working on being more connected with both family and friends in a deeper way.

But the biggest change I made was to take my work beyond movement and into the connection between BODY, MIND, and HEART. My work began to change and so did I.

Three questions began to continuously roll around in my heart and in my mind:

1. Is this all there is in my work and life?

This question has come up for me at many pivotal moments in my life and here it was again. What was it trying to teach me? I had to dig deep and ask myself, "Was it true?" My answer was a resounding NO.

What I was getting out of my life was what I was putting in, meaning I wasn't showing up enough and I was keeping myself small. I felt safe going through the motions, but "What you put into your life becomes the vision of what you want your life to be." If this is true, then I better kick myself in the butt and jump back into my life. "When you change your thinking, your life begins to change quickly."

2. How do I bring fullness of all that I am to the forefront of my life?

Can I be present to the fullness of my true value and worth? Answers poured into me as I spent time meditating and letting them surface, and this is what I heard:

"Slow down. Enjoy the person you have become. You are enough. You do not have to be any different. Appreciate where you are and who you are with. Breathe more. Get acquainted with all that you have. Smile more. Allow yourself to be happy. Re-evaluate harsh judgments, undervalued abilities, and become conscious of the words you use to describe your life and future. Share yourself with others. Ask how can you be of greater service in the world? And lastly, put your attention on others, instead of yourself."

And even more than that…

3. How can I show people more of who I am?

It was this final question that led me on a quest to find an answer.

First, I had to…focus on the expansion of my own presence.

In my Body: I started to anchor in the idea of ALLOWING my own worth. This is not an easy feeling to anchor in. There is so much fear that comes up with the word "worth." Most of us feel unworthy. The question we ask most is "Who am I to feel worthy?" Thoughts and feelings erupted inside me and I didn't like it, and the way it made me feel. I didn't want to sift and sort through the muck of self-doubts that I had, it was easier to keep it down and hidden. I kept coming back to "Why wouldn't I value myself?" I began to practice more self-love and self-care. I practiced kindness with myself, and I began to treat myself as worthy, valuable, and deserving. I treated exercise as a gift to myself, which allowed me to connect with my body, but also, it allowed me to connect on a deeper level with soul.

In my Mind: I began to practice the intentional use of my words. I became conscious of what I was saying and what it meant. I practiced Yoga Nidra meditation daily, which took me out of the overthinking monkey mind and dropped me back into my heart. It allowed me to take a step back and distance myself from unworthy thoughts, and it allowed me to be present in the moment. Sometimes circumstances are not easy. They can be stressful and hurtful, but I had to allow the emotions to flow through me, instead of holding on so tightly. If I wanted to have a different, more expanded life, I had to be present in the words I used, and I had to begin to use better, more abundant words, on a more consistent basis. I had to believe that I was worthy of all the fantastic opportunities entering my life. But I had to do more than that, I had to believe my new vision for my life.

In my Heart: I realized how little time I was giving my heart. Dropping into my intuition and listening to myself it said," I was moving much too fast to even hear the whispers." Then, a crazy thing happened, I started feeling a tingling in the back of my neck. I made sure that I went to the doctor and checked it out to make sure nothing was wrong, but I began to feel like it was telling me something. You have heard the phrase, "he's a pain in the neck." I began to feel the tingle in my neck was trying to tell me something important. Not that I had a brain tumor or something was wrong, but rather something was right, and I needed to listen. I had to start loving myself and it was time to integrate my new truths with my inner and outer life. I had to allow my inner-longings and desires to become actions. I had to re-access my worthiness to let myself have those things. I could no longer underplay my own desires and I began to allow them to come into the forefront of the ways I showed up in the world: for myself, for others, for my work, and for my life.

The shifts in my Body, Mind, and Heart began to reflect through an expanded, hyper presence to my capacities to create.

1. Present to my choice of actions.

2. Present to my use of words.

3. Present to my environment.

4. Present to how I nourished myself.

5. Present to the people I surrounded myself with, people who were positive and expressed this through generous actions.

6. Present to new ideas. Present to new answers. Present to new ways of being more present to even more joy, happiness, fulfillment, clarity, and fun.

We have been taught to look at what we lack in our everyday life. Cultural norms and society have us thinking this way, and the media makes us aware of what we don't have. Negativity is a much easier conversation for everyone, but it pushes us out of alignment with our life.

It is so much easier to fight, complain, to see everything around us that is wrong, and how unfair the world is, instead of the perfect beauty in everything around us. Especially in the things that don't work out. That is the magic of being exactly where you are. The compassion of living in your heart, even when it is breaking.

Presence comes into our world when we are ready to stand still and be in our power. The power comes from being excited to be in this moment and to allow yourself to sit within the moment and listen.

What are we listening for?

Honestly, how often do we allow ourselves to do that?

I know I don't do it nearly enough and I might even say at times, I am afraid to stop and listen. I'm afraid of what I will hear. Whenever I stop long enough, all I hear is the truth of the moment. I can activate my inner hearing and seeing, and I move into what I call my "growing edge." I see far beyond the moment of where I am and expand into my deep feeling awareness. I notice that I must grow in consciousness for my purpose to grow with me.

Who do I need to become?

What gifts do I already have?

What must I let go of in my life to become more present?

We have 80,000 thoughts a day that go through our minds. 97% of the thoughts don't serve us and only 3% are worth listening too.

The truth of all of this: Nothing must change for us to be in Presence, we just need to let go of the story. The story that we have played over and over in our heads, the one that doesn't serve us at all, but keeps us small in our life.

You know the story "I am not good enough." "I have nothing to say." "I don't know how to get money to set up my new business." "Nobody wants to hear what I have to say." I am too fat for anyone to listen to me." "There are no good men or women in the world for me to meet." The list goes on and on about what we don't have. When will we stop ourselves from that boring and overused conversation and move into the personal power, we all have?

Here is the real question we must ask, how can I truly embody "The elegance of being present to my own power?"

The opportunity to be present for so many experiences in our lives. The opportunity to help serve other people. To stop thinking about yourself and start thinking, how I can serve the people around me?

When you are not present you are unable to see your own value. You are unable to feel your worth. You are unable to see your true strength and you are unable to honor the gifts you are here to share.

And, because you are not present to these aspects, you find yourself unable to communicate or speak your purpose and ways you are here to make a difference in the world.

How do these shifts and changes help us create a more dynamic destiny and how does it improve or influence the quality of our life? By being fully PRESENT now.

Here are some steps to allow you to live in Presence:

1. Breathe. Stand still, close your eyes and take a deep breath in for 2 counts, hold your breath for 2

counts, and then slowly blow out the air through your mouth as if you were blowing out through a straw for 2 counts. Try this for 5 rounds. Open your eyes and look around, take in your environment with no judgments. That is being present.

2. Don't take yourself so seriously. We all get caught up in our lives and we forget that everything is not always such a big deal. Take a step back at times and see if there is another way to react? Try to lighten your mood and see if you can be nicer and easier with yourself and those around you.

3. Exercise connects us to our bodies. It is the number one way to reduce stress and depression. Studies have shown that walking, running, Pilates, yoga, spin classes, and lifting weights can not only alter your body, but can make dramatic shifts in the brain. I have always told my clients, "When we feel better, we deal better." And we experience Presence.

4. I find myself in the most Presence in nature. Go outside. Walk, hike and breathe in the trees or the ocean. You will realize how much bigger the world is than you are and drop back into your heart. Stress tears at us when we feel we aren't connected to anything or anyone. Reconnecting with yourself can become your ticket to Presence.

5. Listen to the words you are using every day. Are they empowering and loving? If not, take a moment and take them back. Excuse yourself for the less powerful words and then, replace them with words that are more loving and supportive. Words are powerful, and your body is always listening to what you say, use words that allow you to thrive.

With these steps, I could now see opportunities that were around me that lead me to greater connections with myself and others.

I found I was willing to take risks and I had an unwavering confidence about myself.

I finally allowed myself to receive, instead of pushing opportunities away and I could see the greater possibilities around me.

Your days are your life in miniature. You can experience a renewed love of your life and appreciate the ups and downs on this glorious adventure.

Most of all, in my quiet moments, I am truly at peace with myself and the woman that I am becoming. And for me that is the true essence of PRESENCE.

Conni Ponturo

Conni Ponturo is a leading authority in the field of pain-free living, which includes the power of creating a harmonious connection of mindset, emotions, and body. Respected for her unique approach to Transformational Movement that merges Pilates, Meditation, and Mindset. Conni Ponturo teaches her clients how to flourish at every stage and age of their life. To learn more about Conni Ponturo and her work visit:

www.conniponturo.com

or

www.absolutepilatesupstairs.com

CHAPTER FIVE

THE ESSENTIAL POWER OF BALANCE

Written by Heather Salmon

"As we embrace lifestyles of balance, we open our hearts and minds to living lives of service. As we recognize that all life is connected, we make more conscious choices, taking into account how they will impact the earth and other communities.

When we open our hearts to empathy and are able to be present to the impact of our choices on others, we become part of the solution for our highest evolution."

Heather Salmon

THE ESSENTIAL POWER OF BALANCE

What does balance have to do with living a life of contribution and purpose?

When we are living our lives in balance, we feel a sense of peace with life and fulfillment in how we are utilizing our time and energy. Life does not become effortless, we can still have challenging situations, choices to make and boundaries to set, in regard to how we spend our time and utilize our energy both internally and externally. But, rather than riding things to the extreme and then crashing and burning, we are able to captain our ship and make empowering decisions along the way. When we live a life in balance, we become actively engaged in a multidimensional process that guides us on our way as we navigate the various parts of our lives including work, fun, social and family, as well as personal self-care.

Speaking for myself, to pursue my soul's calling required that I leave a successful Hollywood acting career and move to a Hot Springs in Northern California. For several years, Spirit had been whispering in my ear that I was to forge a new genre of "healing and the performing arts." I had no idea what that would look like exactly, but I knew I was at the forefront of creating a new genre of spiritual edutainment -- a genre that would educate, entertain and be spiritually transformative.

So off I went to Harbin Hot Springs, an eclectic hippy haven, where the likes of Osho, Ram Dass and countless other new age teachers and seekers had communed. While many of my friends did not hesitate to tell me I was crazy to leave a flourishing Hollywood career to wash floors, clean toilets and be a cashier, I saw it as an amazing opportunity to walk my talk and develop my healing and the performing arts craft. After all, they had just finished building a beautiful earthen temple that was just waiting to be put to use and at Harbin I would put my spiritual ideals of community living to the test, as I became immersed in the community of 150 people who lived there and ran the place.

Diving into community living is like diving into a pressure cooker. All romantic ideas of living in community were immediately tested and I got to see reflections of all sides of myself. For me, I have had dreams of living closer to the land, in community, running a retreat center and offering my sacred work, so this seemed like the perfect place to be to polish up my stone and gain experience. I knew I was divinely guided. Harbin was a mecca for spiritual awakening and meeting likeminded people from all over the world, as we hosted over 100,000 guest visits per year.

Therefore, while many people thought that what I was doing was beneath me, I saw it as an amazing opportunity to learn, grow and test out my ideals. Needless to say, my 6 years at Harbin not only delivered all of that and gave me the creative space I needed to develop my vocation as a priestess, and the skills I needed to offer my own retreats, as well as my own unique form of healing and the performing arts. Being there also connected me with some of the most dynamic cutting-edge cultural creatives and gave me opportunities to share my gifts in front of countless people at some of the leading-edge festivals and events. I performed at Burning Man, Harmony Festival, Agape, and I collaborated with amazing spiritual teachers and artists including: Mirabai Devi, Alex and Allyson Grey, Matthew Fox and many others. Most significantly, living at Harbin connected me to my soulmate Donny Regalmuto, who happened to also be the most amazing co-creative partner who continues to exceed my wildest dreams. As Spirit would have it, Donny was not just an amazing life partner, but also an incredible musician and producer. Since 2012 we have produced almost 30 albums, have collaborated on hundreds of sound healing ceremonies and operated a highly successful retreat business from our home in Maui, Hawaii.

Living a life guided by the practices of balance begins within. It begins with a commitment to return to self and finding that still place within, in order to tune in and be guided. In the hectic pace of everyday life, it is easy to become disconnect, overwhelmed and distracted. The easiest, most direct way that I learned to find my way back to my internal guidance system was through breath, centering and shamanic sound healing practices. For years I suffered from depression and felt overwhelmed by my emotions and uncertain as to what my purpose was. When I discovered these tools, I was able to realize and harness a powerful internal guidance system that has never failed me.

Often when we are giving effort and trying to make things happen, we will hold our breath and try and use all of our might. Well if we are in an emergency situation this might serve us well, but on a day to day basis it doesn't. Holding our breath can cause more anxiety, tension and stress.

Conscious Breathing is one of the most powerful things I learned to help me induce stillness and inner peace. I learned this through my yoga practice and by guiding hundreds of women on retreat. Conscious breathing can induce more relaxation very rapidly and more relaxation quiets the mind, leads to stillness and allows for deep listening for truth, understanding and guidance. Here is a simple practice:

Conscious Breathing Exercise

1. Place hands on upper chest - breath into upper chest for 4, exhale for 4; inhale for 4, exhale for 6; inhale for 4 and exhale for 8.

2. Place hands on rib cage...find the breath there. Inhale for 4, exhale for 4; inhale for 4, exhale for 6; inhale for 4 and exhale for 8.

3. Place hands on belly...find the breath in the belly. 4, exhale for 4; inhale for 4, exhale for 6; inhale for 4 and exhale for 8.

4. Leave right hand on belly, float left hand to chest...3 part breathing...Inhale Belly, Dia-

phragm, Chest ... Exhale Chest, Diaphragm, Belly. Repeat for 8 rounds.

5. Rest and allow the breath to be normal. Relax the body. Relax the mind. Feel the support beneath you.

6. Notice the shifts in your energy.

Conscious breathing guides us into an open and receptive state. This is an opportune time to reflect on how we are doing in various areas of our lives. We can create this space as sacred, asking for the highest outcome by offering a prayer and asking for guidance and support.

In this place of inner stillness, we can check in with ourselves to determine what is important and what is really necessary. And within those areas that we deem important, like spending time with friends and family, socializing, self-care and work, we can reflect upon what balance within means to us.

For example, while we can highly value having an active social life, we may also find it important to have some alone time. Likewise, if we strongly value succeeding at work, we may also value having days off just to do nothing or have fun. These things are just as valuable and can replenish us so that we can give from the overflow, rather than from a place of being depleted.

Living a life in balance requires us to prioritize, to set goals and set healthy boundaries with compassion. Our lives become a spiritual vision quest. A vision quest is a ritual in which we seek guidance, wisdom and truth. We create rituals that nurture the sacred space of our body and surroundings. We create connections with the Earth, the Cosmos, our Ancestors, purpose and guides. What we get out of it is a sense of freedom, focus and empowerment to actualize our unique mission that we are here to complete. When we face obstacles or blockages, we use our rituals and the tools of balance to navigate our way through and make course corrections as necessary.

The practice of balance not only guided me to the hot springs where all that I had dreamed and envisioned came together; but, it also guided me to leave the hot springs and move to Maui. This was before the Valley Fires of 2015 devastated the home and town I had been living in. Once on Maui, it led us to clean-up some issues we had with our land and begin offering spiritual transformative retreats that have helped hundreds of women from around the world.

Finding our way to stillness and deep inner listening takes practice. It is something that can be tested as we set our intentions and listen for answers. It is most important to track what we are doing and receiving, as it is easy to forget what you asked for. Journaling is a powerful tool for this. Writing down questions and in-quiries and reporting one's dreams and revelations and examining the correspondence. When we can see the patterns and answers emerging, we gain confidence in the process.

WHAT DOES IT MEAN TO BE OUT OF BALANCE?

We have all found ourselves out of balance from time to time. You know, when you find yourself over-whelmed, frustrated, frozen, hopeless, depressed or powerless? From the age of 17 I experienced many of these feelings and over the next two decades, I found myself going back and forth from up to down. I recognized this as my soul calling me to awaken and pursue my purpose. But I had no idea what my purpose was and would fall back into feelings of depression and despair.

These are classic traits of playing the victim mentality. When we're in the victim mentality, we think that people and life are against us. We become depressed and obsessed, complaining that life is against us and that things aren't going our way. We blame others and project our fears in a never-ending spiral of negativity and wallow in self-pity and anger. We can often become passive aggressive as an outlet for pent up frustration and anger.

In effect, we actually become victims of imbalance!

It is not until we recognize and accept that life is something we create for ourselves that we can begin to rise above the negative spiral of playing the victim. We created our stories and we can change them too and we recognize that playing the victim is actually an act of entitlement, which is a cop out!

When we decide to transform victim consciousness, we begin to take responsibilities for our actions and recognize that life is not against us, unless we claim it to be so! We pull ourselves out of victim consciousness by remembering how very fortunate we are. It is not difficult to take a look around and recognize that if you have food in your refrigerator, a bed to sleep in, clean water to drink and lights to turn off, then you are way better off than over half the people on the planet! According to statistics, nearly ½ the world's population lives on less than $2.50 per day. Over 22,000 children die each day due to poverty. Over 750 million do not have access to clean drinking water. Approximately 1.6 billion people live without electricity. 805 million people do not have enough food to eat. The World Food Programme says, "The poor are hungry and their hunger traps them in poverty." Hunger is the number one cause of death in the world, killing more than HIV/AIDS, malaria, and tuberculosis combined. (source https://www.dosomething.org/us/facts/11-facts-about-global-poverty)

For me, what kept me going was a deep sense of responsibility. Having been the daughter of Canada's first black surgeon as a father and of a mother who worked tirelessly as a civil rights activist, local politician and community leader, I knew I was here to continue the family legacy as a healer and agent of change, even though I had no idea how.

When we pull ourselves out of victim consciousness, we become focused on solutions and become clear about our boundaries. We forgive and move on, raising ourselves up and above our circumstances and we begin to live a life using the powerful tools of balance. We begin to think positively, and those positive thoughts begin to attract positive outcomes. We begin to assert and stretch ourselves, with faith, we go beyond our comfort zone and then we are able to grow and expand. And finding our purpose offering ourselves in service to the greater good, then we find traction and direction!

> "Where there is no struggle, there is no strength.
> Adversity breeds strength."
> *Oprah*

Exercise: Fanning the Flame of Self Love, Gratitude and Appreciation

1. Breath into your heart center.

2. Reflect on something that you are grateful for. Something that brings a smile to your heart...a place you love being, someone you love, something you love doing, etc.

3. Connect with the inner smile. Fan it like a flame with your breath and your intention.

4. Engage all of your senses. What does this memory feel like, look like? Is there a taste or smell associated? Bring it to life!

5. Expand it like a warm light to all of your cells and your entire being.

6. Now, reflect on something you appreciate about yourself. Can be something you've accomplished. Some way you've persevered, been kind, caring, or patient.

7. Acknowledge yourself. Send yourself love and appreciation and an energetic hug or pat on the back.

8. Allow these feelings to expand and nourish you.

"Trust yourself. Create the kind of self that you will be happy
to live with all your life. Make the most of yourself by fanning
the tiny inner spaces of possibility into
flames of achievement."

Golda Meir (Israel's 4th Prime Minister 1969-73)

WE CAN BECOME THE CHANGEMAKERS
OF THE NEW WORLD.

It is vital in this time of the Great Change that women model a new way of being that embraces balance. As we embrace balance, we are bringing about the necessary changes to the world around us. As we create balance within, we create balance without!

The Pachamama Alliance has identified three main areas that are inextricably interconnected and interrelated, as being necessary to shift the world from a

self-destructive direction, to one that is life affirming, in balance and regenerative.

These three areas are:

1. Balance With the Earth - Environmental Sustainability.

Currently we are living in overshoot. This means we are treating the earth as our warehouse and it's running out of resources. Our current rate of consumption is not sustainable, and we are not allowing the earth to regenerate. The rainforests are the lungs of the planet and we are cutting them down to grow crops to feed livestock that are contributing to greenhouse gases and global warming.

2. Balance With Humanity - Social Justice

Issues of social injustice must be addressed. This is also related to Environmental Justice. Areas of toxic waste and mass pollution tend to impact less developed and lower income communities first. The process of colonization has systematically targeted people of color across the globe. Institutionalized racism has existed to systematically give privilege to a select part of the population over others and determines who's incarcerated, has the best schools, opportunities, medical care, etc.

3. Balance Within Our Beings - Spiritual Fulfillment

What we are lacking is our sense of spiritual connection to all of life. That all of life is interrelated and interconnected. As Chief Seattle said, "We did not weave the web of life, we are merely a strand within it and what we do to one part of the web we do to the whole."

We cannot address one of these issues without recognizing that they are all connected and there is work to do within each area.

As we embrace lifestyles of balance, we open our hearts and minds to living lives of services as we recognize that all life is connected. Therefore, we make more conscious choices, taking into account how they will impact the earth and other communities.

We open our hearts to empathy and are able to be present to the impact of our choices on others. We begin to recognize that we are one family here, the human family. That we are one race, the human race. We may be different ethnicities, but we are only one race.

And as we embrace lifestyles of service for the good of all, we become alchemists, able to powerfully transform the world with love!

HEATHER SALMON

Heather Salmon is a renown sound healer, mystic, cultural creative and recording artist. A knowing that we can create a new way of being on Earth that is sustainable, just, and thriving drives Heather. Heather's passion is to inspire change through sharing lifestyle practices that cultivate peace and harmony!

Residing in Maui, Hawaii at the Black Swan Temple, an Eco Sanctuary in the heart of the rainforest, Heather and her husband Donny Regal offer retreats, trainings, and Mystical Alchemy Sound Healing Prayerformances for the healing and upliftment!

Learn more about Heather Salmon and her work by visiting www.blackswantemple.org.

CHAPTER SIX

THE ESSENTIAL POWER OF SELF-AUTHORITY

Written by Patrina Wisdom

"When we are not in our self-authority we lean towards recklessness.

We abandon our sense of worth. Under-estimate our value, and feel disconnected from all that we are.

But, when anchored in the power of self-authority, we consider, discern, and make choices that are in alignment and in harmony with our heart, mind and spirit."

Patrina Wisdom

THE ESSENTIAL POWER OF SELF-AUTHORITY

How has not living in self-authority robbed you of the confidence, relationship, and / or financial abundance that you deserve?

My name is Patrina Wisdom and much like you I embody and share the experiences thread throughout the collective consciousness of women. Essentially, we are very much alike. I am you!

Study of personal development has always been 'my thing.' In fact, I started my journey at 13 years old, fresh out of grammar school and entering into middle school. For as long as I can remember I've absorbed all I could learn about self-esteem, transformation and anything that would move me closer to knowing who I am and who I can become.

And, I believe this study saved my life.

You see, at a very early age I'd already come face to face with a life filled with all kinds of experiences. Some of them incredible, and some of them not so incredible.

My passion for personal development prepared me for these experiences. It prepared me for the pain of my first heartbreak, disappointment, molestation, rape, devastating personal loss, financial hardship, divorce, single parenting, promiscuity, harsh judgment and many other traumas.

I not only made it through all of these experiences, but I came through it all with a pretty good sense of self.

That was until the fateful day on January 6th, 2009. It started like any other day. My husband, 3 kids and I woke up, had breakfast, prepared for our day and around 8am said my "I love you's" to my husband Alex and kissed him goodbye as he left for work.

As I floated through my day full of excitement and anticipation for my husband's return home, I thought it was weird that he had not called, texted, or checked in, but I just assumed he was busy. Then, when the clock struck 10pm, 11pm, and then 12am and I still hadn't heard from him I knew something was wrong.

After a sleepless night of worry, fear, and confusion I was blindsided by an early morning call from the police department and a voice on the other side of the phone telling me that my husband's body was found in the desert, he had died of suicide, and I needed to come and identify his body.

My heart sank to my feet, because on the same day that my husband went missing, I also found out that I was pregnant with my (our) fourth child and I was excited to share the news with him.

In one day my world was turned upside down and would be forever changed. Overnight I now found myself as a single mother, head of household, I stepped into the role of primary breadwinner, and inherited our financial business.

I felt abandoned, scared, alone, unsafe, and unworthy. I had feelings of self-doubt, and I did not necessarily trust myself because I had spent so many years hiding behind my husband and relying on him to lead the family and show me the way. But I refused to play the victim. On the contrary, I was committed to becoming a victor over my situation and turning my tragedy to triumph.

I was especially nervous about having to manage the finances. As an only child of a teenage single mother, we never had money growing up. And although my husband and I had managed to do well for ourselves, I had never been in the position that I now found myself in; breadwinner and steward of the finances. I always had part-time businesses and contributed to the household, but I had never been the sole provider and I never had the responsibility of managing money and paying the bills.

Overnight I came into a large amount of life insurance money and while it was a beautiful gift that allowed me the time and space to find my way, the responsibility of it frightened the hell out of me.

Despite my insecurity around managing this money, I was grateful that my husband loved his family so much that he made sure we would be taken care of in his absence. He forced me to learn how money works and made sure I understood financial concepts, but knowing concepts is very different from applying them.

I spent the first 2 years, after his passing, taking care of everyone else (mentally, spiritually, and financially). I made sure my kids got the therapy and healing they needed. I took time to make sure that our families were okay. I took care of my husband's friends, clients, teammates, and even took over our financial business for two years in an effort to continue my husband's legacy, avoid disappointing others, and make everyone around me proud.

All good things, if my own self-worth wasn't tied to it.

My life had been turned upside down and I lost all sense of self because my entire identity had been wrapped up in my roles within the life I'd built with my husband. And now he was gone. He was my best friend, my protector, my provider, my lover, my everything.

My heart was broken, and I was wandering around like a fish out of water, trying to figure it all out. No intention, no vision for what I wanted to create, no degree or skills to fall back on. I was numb, and on autopilot. I put my feelings of grief, fear, and displacement on a shelf to focus on everyone and everything else and distracted myself from the pain. I was in the space in between my YES and my NO.

As a result, I became reckless. My sense of self-worth was stripped away by my experience and the pain was so unbearable that I would do almost anything to numb the pain or fill the void. Some of my favorite antidotes were alcohol, shopping, traveling, and sex.

It wasn't until early 2013, after finally taking time to deal and heal from pain, that things shifted for me. I woke up one morning and I was complete. Complete with the grief. Complete with numbing. Complete with the roles I'd played out for so many years. Complete with all of it!

I knew I no longer wanted to be in Las Vegas, I no longer wanted to play it safe, I no longer wanted to run my husbands financial business, it was time to go. It was a HELL NO to staying in these roles and a HELL YES to creating a new life.

After a process of re-engaging my personal development and spiritual practices, I finally developed the courage to stand on my own two feet. So after almost four years of living by default, and letting other people's expectations guide my life, I made the tough decision to leave the financial business that my late husband and I spent over a decade building (despite my belief in what we did for families and being a beneficiary of what we did), sold my house and most of our belongings, and moved myself and my four kids from Las Vegas, where I had the support of my family and friends, to San Diego, where I knew nothing and no one.

It was time for me to grow up and step fully into my Self Authority. I knew that moving away was an opportunity for me to discover myself, access and develop my inner strength, and recreate my life. Therefore, despite my feelings of fear and uncertainty, I took the leap.

Within my first 2 years in San Diego I attracted an incredible community of friends, successfully grew my business in personal development, began homeschooling my kids, wrote an Amazon Best Selling book called, *"Motherhoods Not For Punks,"* and had proven to myself that I can take ownership of all of my experiences and use them to fuel the creation of my Badass Bodacious Life! A journey that has beautifully supported me in fulfilling my mission to lead, empower, and inspire other women.

New awareness flooded in...

Self-authority is not given, it's earned. It's something you grow into and developed over time. It's the deepest and truest form of confidence and trust in oneself that is strengthened or diminished with every decision you make.

Each time you honor your YES or your NO you are gaining self-authority.

When you are in self-authority, you feel a sense of safety.

You feel confident, connected and in integrity.

Not only can you recognize and receive opportunities, you begin magnetizing them. You feel limitless and in flow, which is a result of functioning in your highest state of being. In return, you naturally become an inspiration to those around you.

Fast forward to January 2016, after years of rocking my transition (transformation), being fully expressed in my creative and spiritual worlds, taking care of my kids, traveling and loving the new life I'd created for myself.

I had now spent 3 years investing in my business, travel, workshops, coaching and more. Despite my understanding of how money works and what I "should" be doing financially, at the end of the day, I had not been honoring the golden rule of finance, which is to pay yourself first. I was bleeding money.

From the outside looking in everything seemed great! I was the happiest I'd been since the passing of my late husband. My kids and business were thriving, and I had a great community of friends. But in reality, there was one major area of my life, apart of me was still reckless and out of control.

Since leaving the financial services business I'd lost sight of everything that my late husband worked so hard to instill in me. I had no budget, no savings, and no plan. I was living in the moment, spending more money than I was making, and digging myself into a financial hole that I wasn't sure how to get out of.

This was an old pattern of unworthiness that I thought I'd outgrown. I'd been here before. But even after years of healing, growth, and development, building my confidence and self-worth, I discovered a blind spot. I wasn't in control, I wasn't being responsible. My "Scared Child" and old story of unworthiness had somehow taken the wheel again and was driving my decisions, not the "Warrior Woman" that I'd developed into and come to know so well.

After some reflection, I realized that what had changed for me was my dialogue and associations around money. I was in a community of entrepreneurs who spoke primarily of increasing income, scaling their business, and investing in the coaching, tools, and systems needed to move their companies forward. No one was really having conversations about investing or saving. But I think it was because most of my friends weren't in the position, I was in. They were 10 years younger than me on average, had no kids, and didn't own a home.

It was then that I gained a true understanding of how important it is to surround yourself with the right people and I also gained awareness between self-worth and net worth.

In many ways, I felt like a fraud or an imposter. Because despite all of the incredible experiences and friendships I had and the career I was developing, I knew within myself that the fun and the funds would soon come to an end if I didn't get a handle on things. I also realized that my deep seeded blueprint of struggle, fear, and unworthiness was keeping me in this loop of making reckless choices. And it was getting old.

Knowing I can't solve a problem from the same energy and space it was created, I asked myself this question, "What do I need to heal within myself to shift my relationship with money?"

Financial responsibility was an area of my life that still needed developing and I was finally ready to bridge the gap. I was headed toward rock bottom fast when the "Warrior Woman" within me re-emerged and said, "Be more discerning, grow up and stop waiting for someone to save you. It's time to save yourself."

The message didn't come as lovingly as I would've liked, but nevertheless, I got the message and instantly I became a Hell YES to feeling more grounded and in control of my life and my finances. A Hell YES to unraveling the blueprint of scarcity, poverty, and fear that had cursed my family for generations. A Hell YES to ME and MY TRUE WORTH. I was ready to re-write my financial story, but I had no clue where to start.

Up to this point, I was a solopreneur trading time for money, my income was capped, I had no real leverage, and I was a full-time mom homeschooling four kids. There just wasn't enough of me to go around and so I had to be resourceful.

There was a part of me that knew it was time to get back into a financial conversation. I wanted to create opportunities for passive and recurring income, expand time, and start thinking more long term. So, I started looking at online product creation and other ways of creating streams of income that didn't require me to show up and trade time for money. But the online space didn't feel 100% aligned for me because my magic is in person.

After exploring several different options, I hit a wall. So I got quiet, dropped to my knees and told Spirit that I was ready. Ready to stop the cycle of feeling unsafe, responding to life as it relates to money, rather than creating it, and selling myself short. I was ready to stop charging less than I'm worth. Stop stealing from my household to support my business.

I was ready to get out of the business of trying to heal the world at the stake of sacrificing my own health and well-being. I was ready to start building a legitimate and sustainable business that would serve many, create financial abundance, and outlive me.

I wasn't attached to how it looked, as long as it allowed me the freedom to serve at my highest, without compromising my worth. I was seeking an opportunity to trade value for profit and create long term financial independence.

Shortly after having this big shift around my relationship with money, as it relates to self-worth, I was re-introduced to the company and brokerage that my husband and I had built our former financial business with. After seeing the presentation again with fresh eyes, and fresh ears, and as a completely different woman...it just made sense. Timing really is everything.

Re-aligning with this financial company would not only get me back into the financial conversation and provide the accountability I needed to stay on track financially, but I also saw the benefit of sharing this information with the women I serve.

Most women are not comfortable talking about, and/or handling money. We often go from our parents' house to our husband's house. We put our financial futures in someone else's hands. We never really have an opportunity to develop this part of ourselves. Therefore, I saw this as an opportunity to further fulfill my mission to lead, inspire, and empower women. It wouldn't be a total pivot in career, just another tool in my toolbox.

But once again I found myself in the space between Yes and No with this decision. I had invested the last four years and a lot of money building my personal development brand as Patrina Wisdom. I was conflicted, and although it felt so aligned to add financial education and service to my offerings, there were still remnants of fear around how it would be received.

I allowed myself to be riddled with confusion, self-doubt, and a temptation to settle for almost a week before making a decision.

This was a pivotal moment for me, and I had to make a choice.

Would I stay on the path I was on and deny the part of myself that was ready to raise my standards, own another level of self-worth and further heal my relationship with money? Or would I choose to realign with the financial business, pivot my messaging, risk losing or confusing my followers, and develop a new part of myself?

This discovery pointed me back in the direction of personal development. And after loads of thought, journaling, and meditation, I decided to be true to myself and lean in the direction of self-authority once again.

But this was a new level of self-authority because I'd developed an unshakable trust of self, I wasn't afraid to step outside of my comfort zone and risk failure because I knew it would not change or taint the truth of who I am. It was a YES to going it alone if I had to, but I was also very confident that I would be able to gain the support of my community.

In my experience, successful people stand in their self-authority. They prepare and execute on a life plan, rather than winging it or living by the seat of their pants. They are focused and do not waiver in their commitments and convictions. They know and stay true to their purpose and their guiding principles or values.

I created time and space in my schedule to draft a clearly stated mission, purpose and a vision statement that was aligned with my values and long-term outcomes. I came up with SMART (specific, measurable, realistic, time-bound) goals for myself. I then vowed to be discerning and only make choices that were in alignment with my plan. I created Sacred Self-care rituals to support my spiritual and mental well-being on the journey and to maintain harmony between my heart and mind, and then, I took massive action.

As a result of my decision to re-enter the financial industry and add financial education and service to my offerings, I've shifted from focusing solely on earning money, to a focus of earning, saving and investing. I hold higher standards for myself and my family and I feel whole and in control.

My contribution to the world has expanded. My offerings are more holistic because I'm now able to support and mentor women mentally, spiritually, emotionally, and financially.

People who stand in self authority consider, discern, and make choices that are in alignment with their values. They never compromise themselves or settle. And we implement systems and practices that keep us centered and in harmony with our heart and mind.

When you lack a strong sense of self-worth it becomes impossible for you to take a stand for yourself and live in self authority.

One of the guiding principles for gaining financial abundance is Value for Profit.

If you don't value yourself it will always hinder your ability to create profit.

The person who offers the most value always wins!

I want to invite you today to STOP undervaluing yourself and START recognizing, honoring and celebrating ALL that you are. Your voice matters.

Your contribution matters. You matter!

The world has changed and now, more than ever, the world needs women like YOU to let your voice be heard. New models of feminine leadership are being created and there's a place for you within it.

Be more deliberate, make empowered choices, and create an abundant life! This is the greatest gift you can give to yourself, your partner, your children, and society.

Namaste
Patrina Wisdom

PATRINA WISDOM

Patrina Wisdom is an Amazon Bestselling author, speaker, Wealth Mentor, and creator of the Badass Bodacious Life Movement. She believes in order to live a Badass Bodacious Life, you must connect with, embrace, and exercise every part of yourself.

After losing her husband of 20 years to suicide in 2009 and learning that she was pregnant with her fourth child the same day, Patrina Wisdom took her personal story and decades of experience as an entrepreneur and business leader, and began the process of creating her Badass Bodacious Life. She helps Badass Mompreneurs stand in their personal power and create an emPOW-ERed life through Personal/Spiritual/Financial Development, Healthy Work/Life Balance and Sacred Self Care. Transforming busy Mom's lives from stressed to blessed, tired to inspired, and difficult to joyful!

CHAPTER SEVEN

THE ESSENTIAL POWER OF CONNECTION

Written by Dena Breslin

"Collectively, we as women are experiencing an epidemic of disconnection right now. Disconnection to ourselves, our physiology, our hearts, our deepest drives, and needs."

Dena Breslin

THE ESSENTIAL POWER OF CONNECTION

It takes a deep courage to pause, and remove the heavily weighted jacket of doing, of living a life of rapid-fire yes after yes after yes.

The question we must learn to ask ourselves is, "What could open up in my life if I were to say 'no' more often?"

As productive women in today's vibrant and often harried life, we DO MASTER the Art of Calendar Filling, do we not? We fill time with *doing* and very rarely give ourselves time to *pause*. And, we are strategic in naming the productivity: networking, call-backs, meetings, texts, emails, promotions, volunteering, kid's activities, dating, the gym, and social media marketing. However, our *Self* didn't make the list. Things like rest, good nutrition and time to celebrate get put on hold. Often, there is no *art* to these decisions, but rather there is *chaos*. And no one is the wiser. We deflect, avoid, paint a picture of something other than what it is. It's exhausting. Yet, we are the masters of this.

We could easily go as far as saying that collectively we as women are experiencing an epidemic of disconnection right now. Disconnection to ourselves, our physiology, our hearts, our deepest drives, and needs. This is not for lack of desire, lack of doing, lack of yearning, this is primarily a lack of understanding of what true connectedness is. We are aiming the magic wand in the wrong direction, which is outward. We are on autopilot most days -- on the surface insanely 'successful' *or* simply 'insane'. We dodge depression, anxiety, and states of low cellular oxygen from shallow breathing. We are too familiar with wasted time, not enough time, opportunities gone by, mental fog. We often no longer see resources or feel resourceful. We are box checkers. Our relationships are a blur, acceptance without acknowledgment, or depth, whether it is our bosses, colleagues, those we hire, and most sadly, our intimates and children. Five years, then 10 go by. Where am I? Who am I? Our daughters are young ladies now and what have we taught them? Our marriages are devoid of touch, heartbeat, and passion. What is left?

I found reasons to behave in less than admirable ways to get by. The mind chatter was so loud. Music was dull, passion illusive. Dragged myself to move my body, and in some seasons, over exercised to compensate for the nonsense I put into my mouth. I lost sleep, set unreasonable goals, spent too much money, and made excuses for time lost. I saw doctors and took happy pills. It was from this tsunami wave of overwhelm and exhaustion, a cloudy gray emotional palette, almost to the edge of collapse, operating from one cup of coffee to another, that I wondered. I wandered and wondered.

What happens when we are called to raise ourselves up, to stretch our connectedness to something deeper, and we ignore it? When we consciously, or unconsciously rather, choose to dishonor the Universe's request. Oh, all sorts of unpleasantness. I dare say, things such as: disease, loveless marriages, divorce, depression, panic attacks, drug addiction, obesity, insidious cynicism for what is true, a generation of lost children, derailed aspirations, failed careers, chronic low-grade emptiness and broken heartedness, suicide.

But, "being" is nebulous, Dear Universe.
I don't have the time to figure that all out, can't you see,
I'm busy doing, producing, earning, and using.

Ever since I was young my mind thought in body physiology terms. I watch humans, make notes, collect data. I am a scientist, an anthropologist, teacher, and healer. I was stuck in body, sensations, and pain. I was so cerebral and it was costing my spirit. I was great at walling up my heart, for protection, yet, I had no clue it was happening. I talked more, did more, to avoid pause or being alone. I used debate, and knowledge as the catalyst to excel, in fact, to keep myself awake. Yet, I had little connection to my inner knowing.

I lived in the space of rapid heart rate, shallow breathing, spurts of light, and energy, mania, and called it joy. I was super girl. I was a lot of things to everyone else but neglected myself. And as it goes, my body was responding. I craved and ate sugar, in all forms, I slept little, then I binged on laziness. I gained weight, had less energy, argued more, stuffed my real pain by masking it with more time spent on courses, learning, programs, and searching. But, for what? I earned more than I ever imagined possible, and yet carried the same debt as 20 years earlier. I rode the waves of highs and lows, excited to exhausted. I went from relationship to relationship yearning for intimacy, claiming it was my crusade to be better next time, do better than my parents, you know that story.

It takes a deep courage to pause, and remove the heavily weighted jacket of doing, of living a life of rapid-fire yes after yes after yes.

And it seems to me that very few understand this.

As It (the Universe) would have it, in all Its benevolent energy, led me to a place of pause. I couldn't tell if it was my normal come down from a high or if it was an expression of laziness, but it was lasting longer, months vs. days. I began on an odd and unfamiliar path of not doing. And had no idea what it all was about. I wrapped myself up with getting my oldest off to college, so I told myself. I ended yet another romantic relationship, claiming to be "done." I was empty. I was numb. I had no idea I was shedding. I'd never given myself this sort of pause before. It always felt odd, so I rationalized it away, as I had most of my life. This time though, I embraced the word NO. I looked at it square in the face and said, oh hello NO, what are you all about?

There is a healing in this NO.
It was unlike the NO of confusion.
Or, of disbelief in myself or my capabilities.
I danced with this NO.
No to volunteering, no to dating, no to irrational sex, no to courses, and books,and no to drama.
No to what I couldn't take any longer about work, the kids, or the voice inside my mind.

There is an eloquence to the dance with a NO. To understand the difference in how we use NO. How we hear it from within. There is such power in this awareness, such surrender and relief to let NO lead.

Summer turned to Fall and off goes my son to college.

Then, what's this? Breast lump. This is not happening! Oh my God. They took out a measuring tape for this one. My heart raced. Longest week of my life to get that result. Looking at my children that week and my team was like slow motion, deaf to details.

Most importantly, a time of self-reflection.

What have I accomplished in my life?

Who have I been? What regrets do I have?

What will I change if this diagnosis turns out to be nothing?

As it turns out, the diagnosis was nothing.

Yet, it was everything.

It was the beginning of a wake-up call.

It was the Universe's gentle hand nudging me saying it is time to wake-up.

Soon after I hesitantly traveled to Arizona for a Coaching certification I had signed up for earlier in the year. Well, after all, I'd paid for it and so I went. Numb.

No intentions. I said *no* to forced outcomes, I wasn't the leader in this one, I was led.

And while I was there, I heard this master coach, Brendon Burchard, say these words: *"Have you given yourself permission to live your purpose?"*

Permission? I thought, "What does THAT mean? What the hell would that even look like?" That day, we teamed up, in my new friend groups, and rallied through several exercises that forced discovery. I wrote, and wrote and wrote more. WHAAAAA??? is this, I thought. I have NOT given myself permission to be CONNECTED to ME, let alone know MY PURPOSE.

I did not know I was missing a vital piece: GIVING MYSELF PERMISSION.

So, I declared it! And it began to seep into my awareness. I would find out that I was giving myself permission to just BE. It was time for the Universe to align with my being, as it had once been.

Here's the ironic plot twist. That night, following the awakening to this new awareness,

I woke up at midnight with a very strange and very strong side pain. Burning, seemed surface, muscular at first. But why in the middle of the night? Middle of the night stuff is always NOT GOOD. My medical mind reeled, "What is this?? What's going on?" It was relentless, started in my back flank and around the left side clear down to my pelvis. I thought I lifted my suitcases awkwardly. As the hours dragged on and the Ibuprofen didn't touch it, now the urinary symptoms. WHAAAATTT is this?? You are kidding me right now, alone in a hotel room, with a kidney stone? Nah. I'd wait and see. It's six a.m. and I'm still awake, the pain waxing and waning. Advised by my physician father to head to the nearest emergency room, I begrudgingly did what I knew best. Breathing in that Uber as though I was heading into labor and delivery with my fourth child. My mind was replaying every possible reason for this. Was I dehydrated, sure, but no more than usual. Was I jumping around, yep, but that's what you do at these seminars. Was I pushing myself to some energy limit, and what else is new? You play full out. You DO.

I could barely walk into the emergency room. Within 15 minutes the pain was excruciating. There I was, yelling for pain meds. I WAS having this thing! Alone. Myself.

Yet, not alone. I had been placed within the safe walls of modern medicine, of new friends and allies, in a foreign location, but not alone. I felt thousands of years of passion, love, war, power, control, surrender, and adventure surge within me. I felt the Universe in that emergency room on my hand and my forehead.

My yearlong pause had culminated right here and now.

And it was showing up as a pellet sized stone, symbolizing my experience of the past year: pain, process, and release.

The remainder of the week, I continued to recover and participate. But, honestly, it was a blur. There were days of reflection upon returning home, I felt something happening physiologically, mentally, and spiritually.

I even stayed home alone on Thanksgiving, by choice, for the first time in my life.

And, I loved every minute.

In just a matter of weeks, my body had moved through a life-changing doorway that moved me from Pause to Connection, to Freedom.

The fact is our bodies naturally speak to us and I was being urged to listen.

I faced a breast lump, larger than I had ever felt before.

Pre-diabetes diagnosis with high fasting sugars, weight gain, and mental fog.

Culminating with the passing of a kidney stone.

So what did I do? I began to listen to my body.

I wondered, "What resources are there?"

I read. I studied. I learned more. I paused and I listened.

Not long before sugars were under control with diet change. I AM in charge of this, now. Weight down. Blood pressure normalized. Kidney stone passed. I birthed a transformed. What the hell? I gave myself permission to BE. It followed: pause, pain, process, pain, release, pause, regain. ME.

I humbly am you. We are the same friends. We have similar stories, and I may so boldly add, that there's a good chance your story led you to your body's physiology. This, my story, is a short story. Short meaning, it was the first time in almost 50 years that my body had to get involved to send a message. It was loud enough to wake me up.

Some of us have had years of this. Some stories are far longer, some clues harder to find.

WHAT THEN, IS CONNECTION? CONNECTEDNESS TO OURSELF?

This question has saturated my mind since returning home. I believe it may be one of the most important learning we can have in this life. A return to Source. A reawakening of our inner knowing. And, a trust that all things are possible. It is the energy that sustains love and joy and radiates out a ripple to the entire planet.

WHAT PERMISSION HAVE I NOT GIVEN MYSELF?

Then, it came to me. I have not given myself permission to fall in love with ME. And, to be truly honest with you, I never KNEW how important that was. The best description I could come up with was *'Fall in love with me.* Cherish. Respect. Listen to. Be kind to. See myself: my strengths, my truest desires, and my flaws. All those things I was DOING to and for others. While abandoning myself. I SAW it. I FELT it. HEARD it, KNEW it! The flow was so apparent, it flooded me with such a warm light. THAT was joy!

Clarity about SELF connection was surprising to me. My energy was leveled up! Time was flying by, I was in a zone. Breathing deep, heart rate steady. Music had come alive again. Experiences that were once worn out were then renewed. My inner dialogue was so much gentler and nurturing. I could clearly see a new path. I watched as my energy rippled out over my children, my team, and those I never even met before.

I had lived half a lifetime helping others with their health, wellness, performance, relationships, and moving their needle forward. And what I had done in these past months was heal myself. There is a sense now of authentic ease. And, for me that is the genesis of leadership, beauty, power, and success, the core of the feminine within me. It is my feminine heart.

We began this discussion with the claim that we, as women, in this time/space on the planet, are being faced with an epidemic of disconnection, an over giving, an excess of saying YES. This is the conversation, powerful friends, which we have been running from. This is the *mud pie dirt stirring* we have been avoiding. These are the sparks of fire extinguished, our mind's most precious *aha's* forgotten.

To be clear, we CAN and SHALL rebuild the architecture of our lives. We CAN and SHALL create the most important inspired rippling effect of our space and time. We CAN and SHALL bellow the air we've been desperate for. We ARE that powerful.

And this is an inner job and it is quiet and singular. It is not easy, but yet, it is simple. It will take our time, and our commitment. It will push past the boundaries of what we admitted to knowing thus far. It will require silence, demand our patience and our exquisite listening.

We have heard our past, our elders, and our mentors say: love, create, give, and illuminate. What we may not have heard is, "How do we do this?" What we have lost, somewhere around the age of 10, was the most tender awareness of the Gift that we are. Our purpose, dropped in hints by the Universe, one *aha* awareness at a time, in simple joy-filled, fleeting moments from childhood into our womanhood.

Yet, so many of us have been disillusioned to follow a purpose that is not our own. Could you come with me back to a place where you were free, perhaps freer than you are right now? Remember those days? What are your memories of being connected to the deepest of the deep aha moments? When were you most connected to your truest self? Making friends, telling jokes, playing with dolls, being in the midst of playground laughter, playing in the dirt, making mud pies, or cooking with Grandma in the kitchen? What were your best moments? Close your eyes, play back the tape. Take the time to write them down. What do you see there?

It is time to flow from our heart, our most delicate, yet resilient center. As we have created an outward vision, set goals, and crushed them, we CAN and SHALL do the same here, only inward. We will FEEL more powerful than before. GIVE more than ever. Experience more JOY than can be quantified, by standing in our TRUE INNER knowing. No movement, only energy. Falling in love with ourselves.

Are you ready for this commitment?

Let us package this up so we can begin now:

1. Give yourself full permission to BE, to renew, and to fall in love with yourself, NOW.

2. Pause each day through meditation, prayer, and journaling. More than you ever have before. Pull away from all else to hear from your inner voice,

from the Universe, the true Self. Notice the new *aha's* that surface. Notice how you trust yourself. CELEBRATE!!!

3. Create a list of NO: what you are committed to saying NO to from today forward for good, or for a time frame. Say NO far more than you say YES.

4. Take a deep breathe, with an intention to oxygenate every cell. 4 deep breaths in 1 full minute, 5 times a day. Take a look at the human body online, anatomy, cells. And look at yourself anew in the mirror. Cherish that breath, your body, and your mind. Make it your mission.

5. Honor your physical body by learning more about it and choosing healthy whole fresh foods, and quality vitamin supplements. Find the absolute right and most attentive health care practitioners. Seek them out. Get the best referrals. Commit to this now.

6. Move your body more than you ever have. Stretch gently when you get out of bed in the morning. Spend time creating the best musical playlist of your life! Dance, sing, take the stairs, pace when making work calls, stand at your computer, rebound on a trampoline, and walk in nature. What else would you love?

7. Spend time each week in reflection on your Connectedness with yourself, those closest to you,

with those you work with, with those you may not even know. Notice your energy level, notice your strengths, notice your smallest achievements, and tell someone you trust!! CELEBRATE YOU!!

8. Sleep 7-9 hours a night. Plan for it. 5 out of 7 nights minimum.

9. Knowledge is not power. Using the knowledge and learning we feed our mind IS POWER. Read and learn more to enrich your every day. Engage your imagination. Find photography that stimulates your beautiful brain. Read things that fascinate you more than once. Let it seep deep down. Teach someone else.

10. Be keenly aware of who you spend time with regularly. There are new and elevated ways to spend time with inspiring humans. Take inventory to include family. Give yourself permission to let some go. Let people know daily how much you appreciate them. Use words, even if it makes you uneasy at first.

11. Open a savings account JUST FOR YOU. Pay yourself with every paycheck (yes even if it is $20). Be proud of this powerful commitment. Watch your spending by taking notes every day for 7 days. Eliminate wasteful spending in 30 days.

Yes, our heart space is a vulnerable one. But, let it be revealed. Face it.

Master your dance with 'no.' Shed the weight and allow the Universe to breathe life into your true YES!

The feeling begins with you. The work begins with you too.

And, with me. With all of us.

We are ready. We are one connected-ness.

Honor that your heart is what the world needs.

DENA BRESLIN

Dena Breslin, MS PAS, CTCAA, and CHPC, holds 25 years experience in sales, marketing, leadership, and success coaching. A former physician assistant, Dena is still a passionate advocate for holistic and integrated health and wellness. Since 2009, she's been a top leader and founding member of Touchstone Crystal, by Swarovski, the at-home jewelry division of Swarovski, US. Dena is certified by 3 coach schools, including High-Performance Coaching, as taught by esteemed leadership mentor, Brendon Burchard. Her practice incorporates one-on-one coaching, small business, and executive coaching. She is a single mother of three amazing teens, whom she says are truly her best teachers. Learn more about Dena Breslin and her work by visiting www.Myahamind.com and

www.facebook.com/denabreslin

CHAPTER EIGHT

THE ESSENTIAL POWER OF RADIANT ACHIEVEMENT

Written by Christine Howard

"Radiant Achievement is about doing your absolute best to bring forth the seeds of your potential, to bring forth the next level of your own evolution and all your soul is asking of you, to be and become the fullness of the woman you were born to be."

Christine Howard

THE ESSENTIAL POWER OF RADIANT ACHIEVEMENT

What unexpressed parts of ourselves can be realized when we validate and approve of our deepest callings?

There is a cultural issue surrounding achievement that is nearing epidemic proportions – SELF-JUDGE-MENT! Reaching higher and higher levels each year, especially with the social media exposure we subject ourselves to every day, self-judgement is one of the biggest stumbling blocks to achieving our dreams and living a fulfilling life! Sitting in judgment about what we are achieving, how much we are achieving, and in what way we are achieving in our life is a huge disservice to who we came here to be. Self-judgment is detrimental to our commitment to really express our true potential that's hidden in our inner desires. I know this first hand because I too was caught in the trap of self-judgment and lacked my own inner approval and validation to pursue my biggest desires.

For many years as a wife, mother and all-around supportive person, I often downplayed the desires that were calling me. In the rare cases I did take a stand and begin to pursue something close to my heart, I was easily swayed by the beliefs and opinions of those closest to me – including MOI! There were countless occasions when pursuing my dreams created inner and outer tension and I would easily back away from my goal, saying it really wasn't that big of a deal, or it wasn't that important. In these moments, I was really saying I wasn't important! I was on course for an inner personal train wreck! Fortunately for me, it came.

Being gifted with both breast cancer and a painful divorce in a short time frame, I was forced to do some deep inner healing. During this time, I turned over all the big rocks in my life. One boulder was my passion for achievement. Underneath that rock I was able to clearly see the way I had been achieving (and not achieving) many of my goals and desires (especially in regard to relationships) was toxic to me personally and professionally. In working through my stories, I came out the other side with a lot of insight regarding my old ways of achievement and clarity around how I desired to achieve, lead, and live going forward. Shifting from self-judgment, to approval and acceptance of my dreams, desires and what I was achieving, was a perspective shift I desperately needed. Taking this shift even deeper, I learned a completely new way to approach my passion for achievement – that new way is a path of Radiant Achievement. Today I am not only living Radiant Achievement, it has become my life's work.

In this chapter, we will take a deep dive into the world of achievement – what it is, what it's not, and what's possible for our lives when we let go of core limitations related to achievement. Together we will openly look at all aspects of achievement and define a NEW paradigm that is so desperately needed in our lives and in the world. You will not only learn about Radiant Achievement, you will come to see how this paradigm shift can elevate your life to new heights – one filled with joyful achievement and empowered fulfillment. You will come to see how Radiant Achievement is a strategy for transformation and expression of your true radiance. Let's dive in!

You may not realize it, but you are achieving all day long. Moment by moment you are achieving both small and large things. It could be as simple as completing the weekly grocery shopping. Or, as large as launching your dream business. Also, achievement can be even more subtle – like desiring to achieve a state of consciousness where you can hear your self-talk or achieve a place of mindfulness where you can be fully present during a difficult conversation. Achievement is wrapped in everything we do.

When you pause to think about your experience with ACHIEVEMENT, what comes up? Do you have good feelings around what you achieve, or do you feel negative feelings, like sadness or frustration?

To some women, achievement is a four-letter word that conjures up thoughts of struggle, extreme sacrifice, and ego-centered grasping for something to be possessed and held closely. It's the achievement at the expense of everything else in life, including relationships and health. This perspective on achievement can be (and is) repelling to many heart-centered women. Achievement from this view is overly masculine in energy and leaves you feeling used, maybe even violated. There is a good chance that you avoid achievement of your own deep desires with this model.

On the flip side, some women look at achievement as something that is elusive. It sounds great when they talk about it, but somehow, they never seem to hit the target with the big dreams they have for their life. Does this sound familiar? You may believe that if it's meant to be, then it will happen without you getting too involved in the manifestation process. There is a good chance you would like to achieve something specific, however, you just haven't quite figured out how to make that happen.

I want to share with you a secret I discovered... achievement is whatever you define it to be! It can be the overly masculine go-go-go beast that has you on the treadmill 24/7. It can be the unicorns and fairy dust of putting the desire out there and then, patiently doing nothing to make it happen. Or...achievement can be a beautiful journey of growth, joy, learning, letting go, listening inward, etc. if that is what you choose to do. It's up to you!

Before we dive in, let's set the foundation by giving you a couple definitions for ACHIEVEMENT. Per dictionary.com, achievement is *"a thing done successfully, typically by effort, courage, or skill."* Or, achievement can alternately be described as *"the process or fact of achieving something."* In my Radiance Awakened workshop retreat, I define achievement as *"reaching a defined goal or manifesting, an intention."* Sounds simple enough, right? Yes and no!

What **ACHIEVEMENT** is **NOT**:

To create a deeper context for this new paradigm of achievement, it's helpful to talk about what it is NOT, as well as what it IS. It's like looking at both sides of the coin to fully see what you are holding.

As you read what it is not, notice how you feel. Notice if anything comes up physically for you. Do you get any messages in your head? Paying attention to the physical reactions and self-talk is important information that tells us our thoughts you have been operating. These beliefs directly impact your actions, which impacts your results. Without judgment, let's look at what Achievement IS NOT.

1. It is not unhealthy striving to make something happen.

Unhealthy striving includes several elements – how long you work, how fixed you are on things going your way, and how you show up when things don't work out. Striving to achieve includes those times when you are pushing (i.e. trying to force) something to happen, as well as those times where you do not have faith and you show up trying to control too many parts of the process. With all aspects of striving to make things happen, there is an undercurrent of fear and lack of trust – fear that it won't happen when/how you want it to and lack of trust that anyone, but you, can help make your dream a reality.

When you achieve, you do NOT have to push hard. You do not have to work 24/7, forgoing sleep, food and relationships. This is unhealthy striving! You need to find your own limit of unhealthy. Each person is wired a bit differently in how long they can work at something. Feel into your body and rest when needed.

While it is important to be focused, you don't have to push or force anything – not an outcome, not a person, and not yourself. Forcing is negative energy and achievement is about growth and expansion. When you try to force something, you are acting from a place of lack, especially a lack of trust. Use one of my favorite quotes when something doesn't work out "if not this, then something better is coming."

Achievement is not about trying to control all aspects of your goals or intentions. This can quickly become unhealthy for you, as you put yourself in a box. Doing this is stifling and it kills creativity and receptivity! One way for goals to be achieved with grace and ease is to keep creativity open and stay receptive to other ideas and answers coming your way.

2. It is not structuring, strategizing and having it all figured out ahead of time.

Ladies, this is a big one, especially if you were like me. You have most likely heard that every positive trait also has its negative side. This became very apparent for me as I looked at how I was achieving. I loved to plan – vacations, budgets, dinner parties, home projects, etc. Part of it was that it was fun for me – it brought my dreams to life on paper. All this planning also helped me to address my fears of the unknown!

There is a benefit to a plan, but there can be a big downside if taken to the extreme. The downside of detailed plans and having to have it all figured out, is that it is easy to get stuck in planning mode and never get out of the starting gate because you are so overwhelmed with your detailed plan! You don't have to have it ALL figured out! The steps will unfold in their own time.

3. It's not being in your head and overthinking.

When we spend a lot of time in our head, thinking of all the possibilities, thinking of what could go wrong, looking at multiple options, and multiple paths, what happens is that we begin to doubt our decisions and become disconnected from our intuition. Boy can I relate! At one point in my life I was Queen of Changing My Mind. I became paralyzed to take action because I was so stuck in my head, totally disconnected from what my body (i.e. intuition and feelings) was trying to tell me. Not a good place to be!

4. It's not stressing and worrying and wondering if it is going to happen, how and when you want it.

The old model of achievement came with a dark cloud that said you would not succeed, unless you 100% achieved your goal when and how you set out to achieve it. This belief is very limiting! This belief has you alone at the center of the universe – a place you are not!

Clinging to a certain outcome in a certain way and at a certain time is exhausting and creates anxiety – two qualities that are NOT part of Radiant Achievement! I was so good at worrying and so good at changing my mind. So good at clinging to what I wanted and how I wanted it that I missed out on so, so, so many amazing opportunities the universe had for me.

What ACHIEVEMENT IS:

Now that you have an understanding of what Achievement is NOT, I'd like to introduce you to what achievement IS. Some of the things you may already be actively practicing in your life (and quite possibly just not aware of it).

1. It is taking your gifts and talents and connecting them with your inner desire or soul calling to bring them to completion, to life. In my workshop retreat, I share that achievement is when the callings of your soul, your passions and desires, meet the use of your gifts and talents! This is

the cornerstone to meaningful achievement. The "things" you choose to pursue have really chosen you! It's not about sitting and pondering what you should achieve, it's about looking at who you already are and then, listening to your inner wisdom for what you naturally desire to have, do, and be in this lifetime. It's a completely different starting point for your achievement. When you sit still, get quiet and listen, you will be amazed at what bubbles up as a desire to pursue.

2. It is achieving goals from a place of trust and knowing that the way things work out is THE perfect way.

This aspect of achievement says that however things turn out, whether you succeed or fail, is perfect. All goals that are held loosely (vs. the tight grip) open you up to receive ideas, support, and guidance that may alter your goal. What you intended to achieve may become something bigger and better than your imagined because you were open to the flow of universal and divine energy. I have seen this time and time again in my life, as I made the shift to hold my goals and desires loosely. I have also seen that starting down a path toward a desire opens up a completely new path for me to take. This is the power, again, of holding your goals loosely.

Stay in a place of trust that if a door is closed, you don't need to force it open. Keeping your eyes and energy open, trust that a different door (or maybe it's a window or a completely different building) will present itself in time. Know that the way things work out needs to be for your good and all involved, and sometimes when things don't work out exactly as we had planned, it's because it wasn't what was best for us or someone else. I learned this the hard way in my key love relationship!

Trust in what you cannot see. Trust that the next step will appear.

3. It is a way of achieving that allows you to manifest your goals in a fluid and graceful way.

I had to experience this myself to believe it! Not a step-by-step linear process for these heart-centered goals. It is a highly creative and intuitive process. Achievement – in the way we are addressing it here -- is really a blend of tapping into your intuition, being open to receive guidance and answers, and taking inspired action based on this. The fluid and grace happens because your plans are loose plans – you are not overly fixed on having things unfold in any certain way. You are open to ideas, answers and steps being easy! How often do we make life difficult for ourselves, especially when it comes to achieving our desires!

4. It is a way of achieving that supports your growth along the path, where the journey towards your goals is as joyful/ (important/ transformative) as reaching the goal.

Achievement implies doing something you have not done before. Whenever we do something we have not done before we automatically put ourselves in an environment for growth. I like to say our achievement helps us become more of who we truly are at our core – our essence shines as a result of pursuing our desires. In fact, if we are pursuing a goal and experience a lot of pain and suffering, there is a very good chance that we are ripe to learn something new that will allow us to move past the thing that was causing us so much pain.

Now that you have an understanding of what achievement IS and IS NOT, let's look at two issues that have huge impacts on our achievement: (1) *how we evaluate ourselves in our achievement*. (2) *how we measure the worth of our achievement*. Each one of these has a profound effect on our ability to achieve.

How We Evaluate Ourselves In Our Achievement

How are you showing up in the experience of your achievement? When you accomplish something, look at how you respond to your achievement. You may unconsciously put yourself in the danger zone that can actually negate all the work you just accomplished and freeze you from further accomplishments!

Have you ever done one (or several) of these things related to one of your achievements (big or small):

» Compared your work to someone else (most likely someone more advanced), liking their "work" better, totally negating your own work?

» Picked your work apart so severely that it felt as if what you DID accomplish was pretty worthless?

» After completing a task say, "that wasn't so bad, I'm such a loser for taking so long to do it?"

We've been conditioned that there is a collection of *shoulds* that regulate our levels of achievement. See if any of these resonate with you:

» It *should* have happened by now.

» I have invested all of this time and it *should* be more successful than it is by now.

» It *shouldn't* be so hard OR it *should* be easier than this.

Then, there are the ways we take our judgments around achievement personally:

» I *should* be smarter than this.

» I *should* be able to figure this out.

> » I *should* be as far along as others or, even further along.

As mentioned at the beginning of the chapter, judgment has no place in the journey toward our deepest desires. This is especially true for those desires that come from our soul calling. Judgment has no place because there is NO perfect roadmap toward our goals. We are not talking about baking a cake – we are talking about pursuing the goals and desires that are part of who we are. And for that my friend there is no recipe!

When I let go of the SHOULDS I realized that I am already successful (and always have been). I further came to know there are many ways to measure achievement and success. That brought me to consider the question:

How Do We Measure The Worth Of Our Achievement?

This question inspired me to investigate and consider the ways we as a culture measure achievement.

Culturally we've been conditioned to measure the worth our achievements by:

> » How much money we have.
>
> » The material belongings we own.
>
> » Our status in social media and our number of followers.

» The type of work we do and how well known we are for that work.

Additionally, we get caught in measuring our achievement:

» Against another's level of achievement.
» Based on other's approval of our achievement… we look for the high fives, the pats on the backs.
» Society's respect for roles and contribution: (teacher's / motherhood / home based business vs. mega corporation).
» Based on the impact of our achievement in the world.

Getting caught in the cultural norms around achievement can unfortunately cause us to miss the mark on what it is we are truly here to accomplish in our lifetime. We have all seen and heard of people who have achieved the cultural version of success, but they are miserable inside! It shouldn't be a surprise because in many cases, the goals they are pursuing are filled with judgment, based on an egocentric viewpoint. It's an external focus, which means the things they have accomplished are not necessarily in alignment with what their inner self desires for them.

Conversely, we have most likely spoken to people (maybe even ourselves) who had a calling to pursue something, but they never got off the starting block! They (or you) decided ahead of time that the value of their desire was not worthy or important enough.

If you are reading this, I suspect you are looking for a different way to achieve in your lifetime. Let's take a stand to let go of the cultural norms of achievement and success and adopt a higher, more expanded view, which not only serves us, but also serves the world.

MAKE A RADIANT SHIFT TO A HIGHER PATH OF ACHIEVEMENT

There is a deeper meaning and a more meaningful way to measure the success of our achievements. In fact, there is a completely different paradigm for achievement! It is a path of RADIANT ACHIEVEMENT. This path is one of synchronicities and serendipity. This path is a path toward true fulfillment. In order to walk on this path, you must be willing to shift from the traditional achievement model (and all its beliefs) to the model that is Radiant Achievement.

One thing that lights me up - speaking to audiences about making the SHIFT to Radiant Achievement! This lights me up because this shift is such an empowered action. To make the shift to a higher path of achievement, the path of Radiant Achievement, you must be willing to do one profound thing – LET GO! It may sound simple on the surface, but it is deeply transformational and life-changing.

If you are ready to learn a higher, more joyful, more empowered, and more graceful way to achieve, then shift by letting go of the following three things:

1. LET GO of the need for approval from others! No one needs to approve of your dreams and desires, not even you! Instead, take a stand for you by wholeheartedly loving yourself and owning your worth.

2. LET GO of the need to have it all figured out, to see the finish line, and to KNOW everything before you move forward. Instead, take a stand to trust in what you cannot see.

3. LET GO of looking externally for success, happiness and fulfillment. Instead, take a stand to go inward and listen, your inner wisdom and soul and then, pursue that unapologetically.

Making these three core shifts allow you to truly open yourself up to a completely new paradigm. I will say that when I did this, I was able to quickly learn and embody this new path of achievement. It changed how I lived my life in every way!

Radiant Achievement is "traditional" achievement in the sense that you are taking actions and getting results. However, it is different from traditional achievement in that the entire process is done with more MIND-FULNESS and with a DEEP CONNECTION to both your inner and outer worlds. The result is that what you choose to achieve, creates a deeper sense of fulfillment and unfolds in a more graceful and joyful way. This is true success!

The path of Radiant Achievement is an unending loop that includes these three questions:

1. Am I pursuing the things that ignite my soul?

- » Do my actions resonate with my values and deeper intentions for my life? If not, what feels out of alignment?

- » Is there something that keeps calling to me that I am ignoring?

- » Where in my life am I feeling restless, agitated or frustrated? What message is there for me in these feelings?

2. Am I continuing to step forward in the direction of my calling?

- » Am I listening to self-talk that is giving me a lot of shoulds vs. listening to my inner wisdom?

- » If I am feeling resistance to step forward, what growth is wanting to take place if I were to face and work through the resistance?

» What is one small step I can take today or this week to move forward toward my desire?

» What do I need to let go of or start doing to take this step forward?

3. **Am I becoming more of my authentic self as I pursue my own unique path of radiant achievement? Am I expanding into more of my true potential?**

» How do I feel about what I am pursuing? Is there a genuine excitement and joy?

» Do I feel a sense of peace? Is it an inner peace that is telling me I am acting in alignment with a part of my authentic self?

» Am I beginning to recognize more potential and opportunity in myself and my life? Are opportunities coming to me that I never imagined?

» Do I have a growing and deepening desire to stay the course because I desire to see how things will turn out (having fully accepted that I can't see the full impact and reach of what I'm doing)?

» Am I experiencing high creativity and a childlike exuberance?

Staying connected to these three questions will keep you on the path toward YOUR Radiant Achievement. Radiant Achievement is NOT just about the end accomplishment, in fact, it's hardly about that at all!

Radiant Achievement is not about how much or how fast you are achieving. It is about listening to what your soul is asking of you and then, wholeheartedly and unapologetically, pursuing those callings. It is about stepping forward into the unknown. It is about believing these callings will not only help the world, but also transform you in the process. It is about HOW you achieve and WHO you become along that path of achievement.

To sum it up, this is Radiant Achievement:

It is about doing your absolute best to bring forth the seeds of your potential, to bring forth the next level of your own evolution and all your soul is asking of you.

AN INVITATION

I have a heartfelt invitation for you. I know that new information can only impact us if we actually apply it to our lives.

My wish is that this new paradigm around achievement resonated with you as you read it. Whether it seems like the answer you have been looking for, or just an interesting idea, I invite you to try out this new definition in your life. Reflect on the following questions:

» What part of this new paradigm on achievement am I already doing?

» What aspect of this definition am I already doing well?

» What part of this new definition am I resisting?

» What is something I am currently working on that I can apply these principles to?

» What questions/concerns do I have that need to be addressed?

» What am I most excited about? What do I think is now possible for my life by living this new model of Radiant Achievement?

It may seem like a courageous path, and it is. However, you are not alone on this journey of Radiant Achievement. Thousands and thousands of women are walking with you, including me! This is my life work and I would love to continue to support you! I invite you to connect with me. Together we can embrace the power of radiant achievement.

CHRISTINE HOWARD

Christine Howard is a sought-after speaker and innovative business leader. Her transformative products and coaching services, books and talks are instrumental to awakening the radiance and power of women's true beauty and their ability to achieve their soul centered calling. Passionate in her commitment to inspire the lives of women, Christine's work first began during her own transformational heartbreak. Rising from a startling diagnosis of breast cancer, followed by a painful divorce, today she is widely known as an authority on Radiant Achievement teaching and speaking to audiences worldwide. Learn more about Christine Howard and her work by visiting www.thechristinehoward.com

CHAPTER NINE

I AM RISING

"Determine for yourself that NOW is your time to rise.
Then use your voice to declare it aloud.
Declare it with your wholeness.
Claim it with the fullness of your feminine heart.
Step out of the shadows. Claim your truth.
You are an amazing woman.
And it is your time to RISE!

I AM RISING STATEMENTS

Fuel the Essential Powers of the Feminine Heart

I AM RISING…and so are you. In fact, we are all rising every day through every thought, every word and every action. Your thoughts and words are declarations of who and what you define yourself to be and how you interpret your potentials and actions…affirming your personal truth.

Strong positive affirmations – I AM RISING intentional statements – are tools to enhance personal power. They work to purposely assert and direct how you choose to create and experience life.

The key to most of the things we desire in life, whether it's prosperity, career success, health, happiness or true confidence, lies in our relationship with a heightened state of mind. Even more important, is how we manage our state of mind to triumph over unwanted habits and diminishing thought patterns.

THE I AM RISING Intentional Statements provides you a daily practice designed to fuel the essential powers of the feminine heart, sparking shifts in your clarity, confidence and ultimately, unleashing your innate power to rise. With continuous daily practice, you naturally push the edge of what you believe is possible, access new ideas, answers, and directions – all pointing in the direction of your purpose

THE I AM RISING

Intentional Statements
Fuel the Essential Powers of the Feminine Heart
Use of the Power of Your Words

I AM RISING Intentional Statements provide a daily exercise to support you in accessing the power of your words to bring your energy into alignment quickly and easily.

Use of the Power of Your Thoughts

I AM RISING Intentional Statements support you to center your thoughts and prevent you from getting caught in 'run-away' or 'monkey-mind' patterns of thought that deplete your energy and diminish your creative attention.

Use of the Power of Passion

I AM RISING Intentional Statements serve as daily exercises to refresh the powers of your feminine heart and refocus your choices of direction. Your passion will be freed-up to create forward movement.

Use of the Power of Your Breath

As you declare each of the I AM RISING Intentional Statements, become aware of your breath. By creating a practice of being more aware of your breath, you will immediately expand your power to focus. By being present, you are grounded to make clearer choices welcoming fresh opportunities as they are revealed.

Use of the Power of Your Body

The action of connecting breath and body – breathing deeply before and after each I AM RISING Intentional Statement is a dynamic way to anchor in the power of your intentions. This will lead you to a greater connection with your bodies' energy and amplify the power of your presence.

I AM RISING

Intentional Statements

The I AM RISING collection of intentional statements brings together the voices of an amazing collective of conscious women, to move you to fuel the essential powers of the feminine heart.

I AM RISING in my money power.

Today I will create a more empowered relationship with money.

I know my personal relationship with money directly impacts how successful I am.

I will eliminate any limiting beliefs about money that are holding me back personally and professionally.

Developing a good relationship with money will fuel my eagerness, enthusiasm and confidence to take bold new actions.

I am creating the life I deserve and the financial success I desire.

Pamela Plick
CFP®, CDFA™, AWMA®
Certified Money Coach (CMC)®

I AM RISING in the acceptance of my value and worth.

Getting to the place of knowing our true value is one of life's journeys.

When you know your worth and love yourself, your life transforms in so many positive ways.

I didn't recognize or honor my full worth, until my early 40's.

I swallowed my voice, until the day I spoke up.

Today I am valued and self-loved to the ultimate rising power.

This is the only way to get to your desired destination.

Stefanie Grizzelle
Beauty Influencer
Beauty / Life / Wellness

I AM RISING as the Divine Feminine here to shine forth light and love into our world.

My body is a temple and source of creation.

Authentic energy to be honored, respected, cherished, and loved.

I am filled with capacity that is ready to express, ignite, and create dynamically.

I cleanse my heart, body, mind and soul of all that fails to recognize my truth.

Dancing forth as we joyfully rise together.

Jacqueline Bambenek
Holistic Health and Beauty Coach
Access Bars Facilitator and Practitioner

I AM RISING as I accept my imperfections and step into courage and tenacity by channeling my feminine strength.

As I align with my wholeness, I honor my physical and emotional scars, even though society tells me to hide my blemishes and my un-admirable qualities.

From overcoming guilt, shame and blame, I step into my feminine power.

I allow the flow of compassion and love to take over.

I receive peace, love and beauty.

Susan Kastner
Conscious Entrepreneur
Transformational Leader

I AM RISING through the gifts of meditation.

My inner awareness developed over 20 years of meditation has allowed me to tap into more abundance, creativity, compassion, intuition, truth, honesty, empathy, authenticity, joy and most importantly, nurtured the relationship I have with myself.

There is no greater gift than that of self-love.

Meditation is the key to developing more Presence to Power.

Yes, I AM rising with the power of PRESENCE through the gift of meditation.

Tami Roos, PhD
Meditation Teacher, Vibrational Educator,
Best-Selling Author, Speaker and Intuitive Counsellor

I AM RISING in the power and freedom of the recognition that a happy gut leads to a happy life.

I embrace the awareness that digestive health is key to physical strength, to mental clarity and to optimism and joy.

I commit to learning and implementing the simple tools of gut health so I may reap the rewards of a calm, steady nervous system. I am rising in the faith that the diet and lifestyle choices, which insure my gut health, will feel effortless, in time.

Every day, my intention to love and fiercely care for myself compels my health rituals to take root and grow in beautiful abundance.

Julia Loggins
Digestive Health Expert
Creator of The Ultimate Happy Gut Cleanse

I AM RISING as I embody my unique gifts and align in my personal power.

In a society of constant comparison, for too long it has been atemptation to question my own unique abilities and in return, play small and insignificant.

But I have come to see it is my uniqueness that is the very essence of my personal power.

I now know that when I act from the opinions and the desires of others, rather than my own,

I deny my personal power.

Today, I step fully into my power.

Because the world needs me and everyone.

Brianne Dodd
Intuitive Energy Healer

I AM RISING as the creator of the life I live.

I am a creator and I attract through my energetic life force.

I am allowing myself to see and witness possibilities and abundance all around.

With clarity, comfort, and confidence

I am always connecting and offering hope and help.

I am embracing freedom, as I offer my forgiveness for all.

I am safe. I accept myself. I have no fear.

I am resilient and rise above.

I am creating conscious conversations with others, as I vibrantly and enthusiastically shine my light.

My heart feels love. My heart feels peace.

I am content. I am filled with joy.

Lisa Berry
International Show Host,
Author, Holistic Life Coach

I AM RISING as I live my music.

I am Rising.

I am Loving.

I am Kind.

I am Creative.

I am LOVE.

I am JOY.

I am FUN.

I am Happy.

I am Thankful.

I am Warm Golden Sun, shining my Love and Light on everyone.

Now & Always.

I am Supporting.

I am Reminding.

I am Encouraging.

I am leading with Love, Kindness, and Creativity.

Margaux Joy DeNador
Creative Life Balance Coach, Author, Singer Song-
writer and Live Your Music Show Host

I AM RISING as my body and mind are in harmonious balance.

I nourish and fuel my body with high vibrational foods.

I move my body to awaken my inner healing powers.

I sit in meditation to be still.

I surround myself with nature to connect with the healing powers of the earth.

I surround myself with positivity to keep my energies right.

I try to live a non-toxic lifestyle to keep my body and mind clear and free of harmful chemicals.

Yes, I am rising when I choose to live a conscious lifestyle and take care of my body and mind so I can show up every single day to the fullest.

Czerny Hudson
Conscious Mompreneur

I AM RISING as the unique, one of a kind, fearless, confident, *broke the mold* woman that I was put on this earth to be.

I embrace all possibilities and allow myself to manifest greatness.

My words and actions are aligning with my beliefs.

Because of that alignment I am true to my authentic self.

I am loving, thoughtful, appreciative, giving, joyful, fearless grateful, abundant, ready to serve and believe in my values.

Self-care and self-love are the cornerstone of what keeps me connected to myself.

I take obstacles that come my way and use them as stepping stones to new possibilities.

I embrace the joy of being alive and the fun of living.

I respect my body and love it for the journey it has carried me through.

And above all else, I respect myself for who I am becoming every day.

Conni Ponturo
Leading authority in the field of pain-free living and
the power of a harmonious connection with mindset,
body, and emotions

I AM RISING more each day, to meet my natural state of joy.

Upon asking myself the question of intended manifestation, the first thing that I heard was the word JOY!

Focusing on that vibration – rather than a thing – has brought forth some yummy, amazing things into my existence.

Health. Vibrancy. Fun projects. Resources and great friends.

Abundance at its best.

Realizing that this vibration is my natural state of being has allowed me to embody it.

Issabella Rodarte
Visionary Entrepreneur

I AM RISING in my willingness to own and utilize my unique intuitive powers.

I imagine a world where we're not taught to forget what we know.

Where our knowing is honored, valued and appreciated.

Where it's safe to have our gifts seen and voices heard.

Where it's not only understood, but celebrated, that we are all unique and ever-evolving constellations.

I wonder, what would be possible then?

In my life, in the lives of those I hold dear, in our world?

And, I am willing to find out, one conversation at a time, trusting myself, and my senses – including my intuition.

Wendy L. Yost
Intuitive Author, Speaker, Coach and Educator

WRITE YOUR OWN

I AM RISING

Intentional Statement

When writing your *I AM RISING Intentional Statement,* there are two different perspectives you can consider.

The first perspective is to write an I AM RISING Intentional Statement as one that is written to yourself. Here you can consider it as a declarative statement, an intention of a standard by which you declare to hold yourself accountable. In this instance, the statement is one directed towards being and becoming, living and sharing your very best self.

The second perspective of writing an I AM RISING Intentional Statement is one that is written to inspire others. Again, it is a declarative statement, an intentional affirmation. It reflects the acknowledgment of strength you wish to encourage within others.

Here are a few clarifying questions to support you in writing your I AM RISING statement:

» What feminine value do you wish to amplify within yourself or others?

» What sense of personal power do you wish to affirm?

» What strength and creative capacities do you wish to encourage?

» What mindset do you wish to empower?

One final note before you begin to write your I AM RISING Intentional Statement: Avoid using statements such as, *"I will be"* or *"I wish to be"* or any other derivatives of these types of statements, as they are a confirmation of lack. The fact is you truly are already the fullness of your I AM RISING Intentional Statement. You may have not yet discovered it. Or, you may wish to re-affirm it.

Here are a few more examples of I AM RISING Intentional Statements:

» I am rising in my power to transform.

» I am rising in worthiness and wealth.

» I am rising in authentic fulfillment.

» I am rising in happiness and joy.

» I am rising in prosperity and abundance.

» I am rising in my power to lead and achieve.

» I am rising in a sense of creative ease.

Here are a few topics to consider:
» Nourishment
» Creativity
» Passion
» Feminine Energy
» Sacred Purpose
» Unconditional Love
» Sensuality

I AM RISING...

_____

_____

_____

_____

_____

_____

_____

_____

_____

_____

_____

_____

_____

_____

_____

_____

_____

_____

_____

Signature: _____

Date: _____

ABOUT AMAZING WOMAN NATION

AMAZING WOMAN NATION is a diversified education, live event, media, and merchandising company founded by Marsh Engle Media in 2001.

To provide a resource of education and training, THE CAMPUS was established to deliver a collection of fascinating interviews with modern thought leaders; as well as, weekend programs designed to bring women together for an accelerated learning experience, ranging from success in career and business to lifestyle development.

THE CONVERSATIONS WITH AMAZING WOMEN series provides a platform to create new dialogues to help transform the ways we define our futures. The series features unscripted, intimate dialogue with legendary pioneers, authors, entrepreneurs and spirited change-makers, who share inspired ideas relevant to the shifting culture of a woman's lifestyles and her success.

The AMAZING WOMAN NATION philanthropic initiative joins women in a collective intention to create a more empowered future for the next generation of amazing women. Together we aspire to create a world that fully harnesses the power of women, to create lasting and positive change in their own lives, in their communities, and in the world.

For more about AMAZING WOMAN NATION visit, www.AmazingWomanNation.com

ACKNOWLEDGMENTS

Thank you to each and every woman who believed in the creative vision of this book. Your sheer commitment moves me to continuously reach higher.

Thank you to my mother and my grandmother for urging me forward in the 'search for the amazing woman,' giving way to my life's work.

Always and forever, BIG love goes out to my two sons – Jason and Jonathan – to my beautiful daughters-in-law, Czerny and Hanae. And to the precious baby boys who bring so much love to my life, my two grandsons, Jackson and Rio.

Thank you to the thousands of women who have attended *Amazing Woman's Day,* purchase AMAZING WOMAN books and take part in AMAZING WOMAN programs -- from Maui to Montreal, Los Angeles to Toronto -- you inspire me to stay true to my calling every single day.

To the hundreds of clients, past and present, whose purpose and vision are steeped in the essential powers of the feminine heart. It has been my sincere privilege to have the opportunity to support you in some way to complete your most valued mission.

To my readers and friends who connect with me on my Facebook pages, INSTAGRAM, and LinkedIn.

Thank you for the continuous encouragement or for simply stopping by to say hello.

I am forever grateful to the countless thoughts from leaders and authors, who continue to stir my curiosity, make me think, broaden my perspective, and deepen my spiritual connection.

Thank you to my valued mentors, colleagues, consultants, mastermind partners, publisher and agents.

And, to my cherished friends, thank you for bringing so much inspiration, love and sheer joy into my life. Your stream of encouragement never fails to move me. And your friendship motivates me.

Yes, we are rising, together!

ABOUT MARSH ENGLE

Marsh Engle is a pioneer and leading authority in the field of women's success, bridging creativity, personal power and achievement. A multi-published author of the AMAZING WOMAN book series and award-winning entrepreneur, her work and multi-decade research, promotes practices that lead women to achieve with influence and impact.

In 2016, Marsh served as an elected delegate to THE UNITED STATE OF WOMEN, an acclaimed leadership program led by First Lady Michelle Obama. Marsh has shared the stage with bestselling authors including, Don Miguel Ruiz and Marianne Williamson; International Fashion Designer, Michelle Bohbot; Acclaimed

Journalists Maria Shriver; and, stars from television and film.

> "I believe in the creative power of women. We have the
> unique ability to make the world a better place."

In 2011, just after 911, Marsh Engle was among the few writers who were trusted to enter the firehouses of New York City. Her role was to interview and document the stories of the fewer than 25 women who serve among the FDNY. The women whose life stories she was entrusted to tell were the first women – 25 out of 12,000 firefighters – to serve in the 114-year history of firefighters in New York City.

> "These women are true pioneering, trailblazers. They
> changed the history of firefighting in NYC. They opened the
> door to a new way of interpreting possibilities and potentials
> for themselves and for other women. And, in doing so they
> changed the destiny for women in firefighting and beyond."

The stories of the women firefighters of FDNY are published in AMAZING WOMAN AMAZING FIREFIGHTER (2002).

Marsh Engle's book, THE SACRED AGREE-MENTS: *Purpose. Passion. And, the Power to Lead* (2017) is based on her celebrated course, moving thousands of women to liberate their innate power to create purpose-driven change in their lives. In this book, Marsh shares useful insights that have guided her 20+ years of coaching over 25,000 women and inspires readers to rise in higher creativity to achieve with influence and impact.

DEAR AMAZING DAUGHTER (2018) written by Marsh, along with a collaborative team of women contributors, brings to light the power of purpose-driven conversation to create transformational shifts in their lives and in the lives of the future generation of amazing women.

AMAZING WOMAN NATION, founded by Marsh Engle in 2001 is devoted to enhancing the lives of women by designing lifestyle content, training programs and products positioned to impact millions. The organization is powered by MARSH ENGLE MEDIA, a diversified, cross-platform media production company.

Acknowledged as a distinctive authority in the field of consumer communications and brand enhancement, her clients have included, Paramount Pictures, Viacom, Children's Television Workshop, Australian Broadcasting and more. Her productions have been seen by hundreds of thousands across the United States, including those at THE WHITE HOUSE.

Since 1999 her philanthropic contributions have supported leading organizations including, DARE

(Drug Abuse Resistance Education), RAINN (Rape, Abuse, Incest National Network), Susan G. Komen Breast Cancer Foundation, National Center for Missing & Exploited Children, CARE, YWCA (Eliminating Racism. Empowering Women), Dress For Success (Empowering women to achieve economic independence) and Safe Passage.

For more information about Marsh Engle visit

www.MarshEngle.com